Love, Light

How to move fo
the unthinkable happens

By

Lauren Rosenberg

Published by

i2i Publishing. Manchester.
www.i2ipublishing.co.uk

ACKNOWLEDGEMENTS

I would like to thank my family and friends and all of those who supported and advised us, including my therapist colleagues and trainers, the legal team, rabbis and other religious leaders, my children's friends and teachers, the first responders and those around the world who we don't know but who prayed for Liora and did amazing things to help. May you continue to spread unconditional love.

As a result of this sudden tragedy, people all over the world spread unconditional love and supported each other.

DEDICATION

For Liora

In memory of our beautiful daughter.
May your light and love shine forever.

DISCLAIMER

Please note that Modern Energy Techniques are not replacements or substitutes for traditional medical treatments but should be considered as complementary and supplemental to it. Under no circumstances should you cease taking prescribed medication without your doctor's guidance and approval. The information in this book is not intended as medical advice.

CONTENTS

FOREWORD

Lauren – in her bravery as a mother and dedication to move on for the sake of her husband and daughters from the devastating loss of her beautiful, talented and inspirational daughter Liora – has found the courage to write this incredibly touching and helpful book in order to give hope to others who have suffered such a tragic loss.

I had the privilege of spending time with Liora: as her name suggests, she was a beautiful light. Rarely do you find a teenage girl who was so caring of others. She was inspired to study healing modalities in order to help her peers.

After bravely recounting the story of Liora's last days in the first few chapters, Lauren then shares several powerful mindfulness, energy and affirmation techniques to enable readers also to take these important steps to help themselves and their families continue their lives and rejoice in the life of a lost loved one.

With the love, skills and caring Liora demonstrated in her short life on this planet, I'd like to think of her now helping young souls in the dimension where she now exists.

Lots of love to you, Lauren, and your family.

Karl Dawson
Hay House Author
Creator of Matrix Reimprinting
EFT FOUNDING MASTER

Made by Simmy More

INTRODUCTION

I'm Lauren Rosenberg, an international fear and phobia relief expert, qualified holistic therapist, Reiki master and practitioner, mindset expert, trainer and energist.

In April 2016, my world was turned upside-down when the unthinkable happened: my beautiful, radiant 20-year-old daughter Liora died unexpectedly.

The name Liora in Hebrew means 'light for me'. Ora is not just a simple light but a bigger one, a bright light that brings redemption and happiness to all who see it. Liora certainly brought redemption and happiness to numerous people around the globe. A Facebook support group attracted over 15,000 people when she was in hospital.

She was, and is, our light and helps me now by illuminating my thoughts and bringing them together in this book, which I hope will help you.

What I feel compelled to share is how I have coped with this terrible, tragic event and been able to move forward to continue to create a purposeful and meaningful life for myself and my family. I'm not saying this has been easy. Liora's sudden passing was devastating. I have cried a lot and gone through the normal range of emotions. She was my eldest daughter and I had a very close relationship with her. We had common interests in energy work and personal development.

There were times at the hospital – and since her death – when I just wanted to give up. That means I can empathise with those who feel they can't cope with everyday life when terrible things happen. I understand their desire to shut themselves away and withdraw from society for a short while and sometimes permanently.

But I believe that if I allow Liora's passing to hold me back, keep me stuck and stop me from living my life fully, it would be a waste of my life.

I also don't want our other four girls, currently aged 22, 21, 17 and 12, to be defined by this tragedy so they're forever remembered as 'the sister of that lovely girl who died.' I want them to enjoy full and meaningful lives as would Liora – she never would have wanted us to stop living in memory of her because she always lived her life to the full.

I have had many messages via Facebook and text encouraging me to share my thoughts and actions and telling me that I am an inspiration to others, although I've never thought of myself this way before.

The truth is that I don't know how I would have managed without knowing how to use energy healing and similar tools to cope and that's why I decided to write this book. I know that it would be even more difficult for someone to handle loss and grief if they didn't know how to help themselves and those around them. This feels especially important at the moment, because everywhere I turn, it seems as if people are experiencing what seem to be insurmountable challenges in their lives. Indeed, I haven't been free of challenges myself. As well as Liora's passing, I've had other challenges to deal with, including a carjacking.

But it's different for me – I have been given the opportunity to become an energist, and that means I'm able to use many tools not only to help myself but those around me too. These tools have turned out to be extremely useful, even life-changing, and they've given me, my family and friends much positive energy to draw on after Liora's passing.

My friends and clients who have used these tools on a consistent basis have made significant positive changes to their lives too, and I believe you can do the same.

Of course, I'm not suggesting that these tools alone will solve all your problems; after all, this journey called life is ongoing. But I know that by using them I've been able to cope and survive the unthinkable and turn negative life experiences into positive ones.

It is my sincere wish that you too will want to incorporate some of the tools I use into your own life, so you can develop a better understanding of who you are. I also want you to be able to enjoy happiness, love and tranquillity so you can move forward from where you are now to a better place in your life.

The principles in this book will help you refocus your life and concentrate on the positive. They will help you discover new ways to deal with any problem or situation you're facing (or may face in the future). By using these techniques, you'll be able to enhance your life and achieve more, whether you have been affected by unexpected dramatic events or not.

I hope the perspective you gain from learning a different approach to what happens around you will give you clarity, a sense of purpose and a more positive outlook on the future so you won't be stuck in a place of anger and resentment. Like me, I hope you will learn how to turn your anger or sadness into love so you can feel more in control, be happier and feel more able to cope with the unthinkable.

I believe that my training in Modern Energy Tapping, Colour Therapy and Positive Mindset helped to prepare me for the work I needed to do with Liora in the hospital. By using the techniques shared in this book (and making use of the legal system), and with the help of my family and friends, we were able to keep Liora alive for 12 days after the doctors wanted to turn off her life-support machine.

Not only did she have those extra days, I was also able to learn how to live my life again after she left us. Now, I want to show you how to use these tools and techniques to help you through your life.

So, whether you too have experienced the death of a loved one, suffered a traumatic relationship breakdown, found yourself unemployed or are struggling in some other way to cope with other changes in your life, please read on and let me show you how you can move forward with positivity to create a life that is rewarding, joyful and meaningful.

These techniques aren't just for coping with traumatic events, so even if things are currently going well for you, you'll be able to benefit from this book and make things even better for yourself. No matter how good life is right now, we know we'll all experience loss, grief, anger and disappointment at some point in our lives. The problem is that we aren't generally told how to deal with these powerful emotions or how to move forward from disappointment and loss.

What I've learned from my own tragic experience is that anything is possible. None of us should limit ourselves. We all have a choice in what we do and how we react to what goes on around us. Trauma often comes out of the blue, like a lightning bolt, as it did for our family, and that can lead to feelings of powerlessness and loss of control.

But even if we can't change the events around us, we can choose how we respond to them. We can choose whether to be victims and remain helpless or to take action and move forward to a better life. We can't hide from life's difficulties and we will never be ready for painful experiences, but we can learn to deal with them better.

Liora's passing has been hard to bear, but I have chosen to build and maintain a positive outlook on life by choosing to be happy and positive. This approach is powerful because it allows me to show my other children how good life can be and that they can still enjoy a good life, even though they've experienced tragedy.

Liora's passing has taught me how important it is that we each take time to appreciate those we care about, and to show them that we care. It's easy to forget this, so there's a section in this book that will help you think about this too.

When you read our story, it will be clear that my family follows the Jewish faith and believe in Divine Providence. This book doesn't suggest, however, that you must follow a certain religion to be happy or indeed any religion at all. My objective is to bring you to the conclusion that, by strengthening your faith and trust, you can look forward to a happier life and move forward, even if you have suffered a traumatic loss or event.

I believe that everything is for the best. Life is easier if we accept that our path in life has been predetermined. I was given the beautiful, perfect gift of Liora in 1996 and I am grateful for the 20 years I had with her. Now, her path means she's not physically here with me on earth; she is needed elsewhere, but her energy never dies.

After going through the experience of Liora's sudden illness, my best advice to you is to remove any anger, resentment and sadness from your heart and replace it with unconditional love. In the following pages, I will show you how to do this.

To get the most from this book, you will need to be open to new ideas and possibilities – often ones you may not have considered before. It's important that you're willing to work on yourself and unlock your limiting beliefs and be open to accepting the support of others.

To make changes we must have some step-by-step plans for altering the way we think and feel. If we want to move forward with our lives every day, we need to get out of our comfort zone. I hope you'll choose to do this and that your journey will be exciting, successful and filled with love, joy and happiness.

Above all, remember life is a voyage of discovery. We all gather experiences that can help us move forward even if they seem negative at the time. So, start from where you are and use your previous experiences to help you.

Life is full of ups and downs; sometimes it feels like being on a rollercoaster. But it's important to keep moving forward, otherwise you'll stay stuck or go backwards, and that's no way to live a full life.

'I believe there are no accidents in our universe. Every meeting and every event is orchestrated by a divine force. Low points are there to teach us to propel ourselves upwards.'

Wayne Dyer

As well as learning about key techniques and tools in this book, you can also access further resources via my website (see page 188) and the closed Facebook group (see page 176).

But before I move on to share some of the tools and techniques you can use to help yourself, let me first set the scene by sharing my experience of '*When the Unthinkable Happened*' and tell you a little more about Liora and her impact on the world.

PART 1:
LOVE

CHAPTER 1
WHEN THE UNTHINKABLE HAPPENED

Have you ever had a day when you just wanted to give up, when things seemed so bad that you just didn't know where to turn or what to do?

That's how I felt on 19 April 2016.

My husband and I were in a hospital waiting to get news about our daughter. A middle-aged consultant we'd never met before approached us and said, 'Mr and Mrs Rosenberg? Could you please follow me? We need to talk in private.'

Instinctively, I knew something was wrong because it's never good news when a doctor asks to talk to you in private.

We followed the consultant along a stark, white corridor that seemed to go on forever. He stopped and looked into each room as we passed, trying to find one that was empty.

The clinical smell of the disinfectant filled our nostrils and hordes of people passed us, but they were just a blur.

I noticed that Stuart, my husband, was very pale. I was shaking because I was terrified; I had no idea what was going to happen next.

At last, we were gestured into a large, bright room. It had massive windows and I remember noticing that I could see the Shard and the Sky Garden building through it.

The room was full of white tables and chairs; it felt cold and impersonal. It looked as if it was used as a Day Room for outpatients; it felt huge and empty with only the three of us in it.

Stuart and I sat down at a table and the consultant took a seat opposite.

At that moment, I became aware that I was still wearing the same clothes I'd put on the previous morning: a black skirt, a blue long-sleeved top and a black cardigan. My hair was unbrushed and my clothes were creased. I hadn't slept for 48 hours.

The consultant began to speak.

'I'm sorry to have to tell you that your daughter will die tonight,' he said, with little tenderness.

There were a few minutes of eerie silence. We were in disbelief.

'Is there nothing you can do? Are you sure?' gasped Stuart. He was clearly in shock. I was worried he might collapse at any moment.

My husband asked lots of questions; after all, only hours before we'd been told that our daughter was going to be fine.

I couldn't talk. I felt paralysed with shock. My beautiful daughter was going to die. How could that be? Everything felt completely surreal; I just couldn't believe this was happening.

Just 48 hours before, everything had been so normal. Sunday had been Stuart's birthday and we'd all had a lovely day celebrating together.

In the morning, I'd gone to the shops with Liora. Everywhere we went she bumped into someone she knew: old school friends, her cousins and some of my very close friends too. Nobody knew that was going to be the last time they would see her.

The house was a bit of a mess that Sunday because we'd had a water leak and we were having some building work done. Everything was piled up in the wrong rooms, but we managed.

When we got back from the shops, our Hendon home was filled with the gorgeous smell of the birthday cake as it baked in the oven. All five girls – Judy (then 18), Fiona (17), Adina (13), Miri (8) and Liora – were all laughing and joking together. Our two dogs joined in the fun too.

At 20, Liora was the eldest of our girls. She was a talented artist, teaching assistant and, at the time she qualified, the youngest energist in the UK. Liora was full of life; always coming up with new ideas for products for my holistic business and for her own creative projects.

We had a lovely meal together, eating in the dining room rather than at the kitchen table because it was a special occasion.

We sang Happy Birthday and the girls gave Stuart presents. We were in good spirits; we had no idea what was about to happen.

Monday 18 April

I remember this day well. It was a coldish rainy Monday and the start of the Easter school holidays. I took Judy to her extra biology lesson as she was preparing for her A-Level exam. Then, while Liora was still sleeping, I took her black Nissan Micra to the garage because it seemed to have a flat tyre.

Liora loved her car. She had pink mats inside and a pink plastic flower on the dashboard that danced as she drove. She had saved up for the car herself and it was her little baby. She hoped that one day she would be able to upgrade to a Nissan Juke.

As an energist, I know that when your physiology isn't working correctly, everything around you is affected; the world is simply a reflection of how you feel. Your energy reflects back so you know when you need to take care of yourself. Once, a pain in my chest coincided with my car not starting. Maybe the problem with the car should have alerted me to the fact that something was wrong, but it didn't.

Judy came home from her lesson and Liora and I went for a mid-morning coffee in the lovely warm Starbucks inside Sainsbury's. Liora much preferred working there than at home because she loved the atmosphere. She was a familiar sight with her laptop and Coffee Light Frappuccino®. She went there so often that some of the staff knew how to make her drink just the way she liked it, with an extra shot of coffee and lots of ice.

While we sipped our drinks, we talked about the work we were doing together and chatted with the staff. Liora looked great, as usual. People used to say that she could have been a model. She dressed fashionably and took time over her hair and make-up, which was always perfect because she was a qualified make-up artist.

Liora loved the ambience in Starbucks. It was bright, spacious and very friendly. She was chatty and often talked to the staff and other customers when she was there. They used to tell her their problems. Sometimes she would talk to them about things that were making them unhappy and she'd encourage them to make changes and move forward with their life. One person even left and started a new career as a result of talking to Liora.

At lunchtime, I took Fiona and Adina to eat out at a nice restaurant near home. The girls were happy as they ate their burgers, chips and hot dogs. Liora didn't come because she wanted to work on her latest art project. She was doing a black and white painting titled 'Happiness is Made from Home'.

At around 3pm, Liora, Adina and I went to Tiger, an art shop in Finchley, to buy materials for the projects they wanted to work on over the Easter holidays. They bought canvases and paintbrushes, full of joyful anticipation as they looked forward to using them.

Liora loved to browse around Tiger because it always had lots of interesting and colourful things to look at. Little did I know that this would be the last time I would be shopping with my daughter.

Next, I took Miri to her favourite gymnastics class at the sports centre. I usually stayed and watched, but this time I didn't. I went home and chatted to Liora about the artwork she was planning to create. It was a normal day and I was just a normal mum playing taxi service to her five girls who were all busy with their activities.

Later, I went with Fiona to collect Miri from her class and Adina was at home with Liora. While I was driving, Liora left a message on my mobile: 'Je ne me sens pas bien, Maman,' she wrote, 'I don't feel well, Mum.' I'm French, so she often spoke to me in my native language, something she did extremely well and with an amazing accent.

When I got home at about 7pm, Liora said she had tummy ache and wasn't feeling great. She'd tried using colour therapy (see page 115) to make it go. It usually worked for her, but this time it didn't.

About an hour later she started to get slightly confused. She was uncomfortable and in pain; she started to get agitated. This was very unlike her. She started saying things that didn't make sense.

I called Hatzola, a fast and free volunteer team who respond to medical emergencies and casualty incidents in the community.

Two paramedics arrived in a car and checked her over but couldn't find anything wrong. But she was confused, and something didn't seem right, so I asked them to take her to hospital. The paramedics requested a Hatzola ambulance from their Golders Green garage. By now it was about 8pm.

As they strapped Liora into a mobility chair she started to get even more unwell. We were shocked and petrified because she had never been like this before. Then I remembered what my energy teacher had told me to do in a case like this and I started working on her using Modern Energy Tapping techniques (see page 101). I wanted to release any blockages in her energy flow and minimise any damage to her body.

The crew secured Liora on the bed in the ambulance and Stuart and I sat further up. From where we were sitting, I could just about reach Liora's hand. The ambulance crew seemed to drive extremely fast. Liora remained agitated in the ambulance. It was so disturbing to see our daughter like that. I imagine you'd feel the same seeing someone you love in the same situation.

When we got to the Royal Free Hospital, the ambulance crew registered Liora and passed on their observations to the nurses and doctors. They were amazing, taking all the pressure off us so we could concentrate fully on Liora.

We went into an assessment room and a nurse inserted a cannula into Liora's arm to make it easier to take blood and do tests.

Liora was still confused. At first, she thought she was at the doctors' surgery. She didn't want to be there. They were trying to put in a catheter but Liora said she wanted to walk to the toilet herself. Of course, they couldn't let her do that.

I think they sedated her at that point. The doctors seemed to think she'd become diabetic, so they were running tests to check this. Liora was hooked up to a lot of machines. I remember looking at all the tubes and numbers and listening to all the bleeping sounds they made. None of it made any sense to me. It was a horrible, bewildering scene and I was very anxious.

Nothing can prepare you for the shock of a situation like this. Stuart and I both felt totally vulnerable and lost. We had endless questions and no answers. We scrutinised the faces of every doctor and nurse who came to see Liora, hoping for an indication of what they were thinking. We were hoping they'd be able to explain what was going on. We just wanted them to tell us that everything was going to be alright.

Later that night, Liora was taken for a chest X-ray as well as a number of other scans. I held her hand as they pushed her through the corridor to the X-ray area, although I couldn't go into the room with her.

Then suddenly, doctors and consultants were rushing down the corridor, their white coats flapping as they ran.

I instantly knew something was seriously wrong. Later, I found out that while she was having the scans, Liora had vomited.

I was trying to get into the room, but someone that the hospital had sent to look after us was there to stop us. She tried to calm us down and distract us.

At that point, we had no idea what was wrong. Tears were streaming down my face. But all Stuart and I could do was stand in the corridor and hope everything would be alright.

What we didn't know at this point was that Liora had aspirated when she vomited. In other words, she had breathed her own vomit into her lungs. It was this event that was to have a critical impact on her ability to recover.

Eventually, the medical staff asked Stuart and I to go into a small room near the Intensive Care Unit.

A female doctor said: 'Your daughter has a tiny bleed on the brain. We're not sure of the damage but she needs to be transferred to another hospital.'

Then they wheeled Liora out of the X-ray room and attached her to a respirator to help her breathe.

As this was happening, I was suddenly reminded of an episode of EastEnders that I'd watched with Liora (we used to watch it together late at night on my iPad). In this specific episode, I recalled a storyline where a baby was diagnosed with a bleed on the brain and how the family had to wait months to see if the baby was going to get better. I imagined it would be the same for us.

By now we were in a tiny waiting room with two chairs. I stood, but Stuart was feeling faint. He needed to sit with his legs raised to stop him from passing out. I felt I had no choice but to be strong for everyone.

We were then informed that, because she had aspirated her vomit earlier, Liora had now also contracted pneumonia.

At around 2am, my friend Chagit Kramer arrived at the hospital. I was amazed to see her. I'd called her earlier in the evening before I contacted Hatzola to see if she knew a private doctor who could come out to see Liora.

Despite having a 19-year-old and 14-year-old triplets, she'd phoned our house again later to see how Liora was doing. When she found out, she decided to come to the hospital to see if we needed anything.

She stayed with Liora when we had to go into another room to speak to the consultant. We took a photo of Chagit with Liora so we could show it to Liora when she was better. I was pleased that Liora wasn't alone, even though she didn't seem to be aware of what was going on around her.

The consultant explained that Liora would be transferred to a neurological ward at the Royal London Hospital as the Royal Free no longer had a specialist ward.

I waited to go with Liora in the ambulance. Chagit said she would give Stuart a lift home so he would have someone to talk to rather than being on his own. Chagit was a blessing. Having her with us, I didn't need to worry about my husband because I knew Chagit would support him.

It took over an hour to prepare Liora for the transfer. All this time, I kept on talking to her and checking to make sure everything was done correctly. There was a lovely nurse with us who was very meticulous. She noticed that a piece of equipment in the first ambulance didn't have enough battery life to last the journey to the next hospital, so she requested another ambulance. She was very concerned about what might happen if we got stuck in traffic.

It was the early hours of the morning when we left the Royal Free. I was able to go in the ambulance with Liora. At that point, I called our friend Richard to ask him to collect Stuart from our home and drive him to the Royal London in his car.

Although the ambulance seemed huge, I wasn't allowed to sit beside Liora, who was attached to a lot of machines. The driver was very experienced, friendly and caring. He was very skilful at driving at speed and be able to go through red lights when he needed to, with the emergency flashing blue lights.

As a driver, you instinctively stop at red lights, of course, which is why it feels so freakish when the ambulance goes straight through them. For some while afterwards, whenever I saw flashing blue lights, I would get panicky and upset because it took me back to the time when I was in the ambulance with Liora.

It happened one day when I was taking the girls to school, and I just burst into tears. I knew I had to do something, so I worked on myself using Modern Energy Tapping. Because of this, I now don't panic or get upset when I see an ambulance on an emergency call. I simply send love and healing to the people who are being rushed to hospital.

Tuesday 19 April

By the time we got to the Royal London, it was Tuesday 19 April. As soon as Liora arrived, they started to do an initial assessment. We were in a large room where there were lots of patients. The ambulance crew spoke to the hospital staff, but it was all in jargon I didn't understand.

Liora was attached to machines that belonged to the Royal Free, so everything had to be swapped over. She even had to be moved to a new bed. I watched as they moved her. Then the neurologist came in and ordered a CT scan.

I remember strange details about everything that happened. My phone needed charging, so the nurses let me plug it in next to their desk. When they took Liora for the scan, I rang Stuart to update him and ask how our four other daughters were doing. It was so difficult. I needed to be with Liora, but I was also concerned about how my other girls were coping.

After the CT scan, the consultant said, 'Don't worry, it's just a little bleed on the brain, she should be okay.'

I was so relieved. The consultant told me she was stable and that there was no need to do another CT scan, so they'd just transfer her to a room in Intensive Care. The consultant left and said she'd see us later. They moved Liora to the ward at around lunchtime. They said I couldn't go in because they needed to set her up, assess her and do a handover to the new team. Lots of relatives of other patients were waiting patiently in the corridor. I demanded to go in, but the staff said I couldn't. After waiting a while, I just barged in. I think they were rather taken aback. Maybe it was my French character coming out because I was determined. I said, 'She's my daughter and I'm coming in.' They didn't try to stop me.

I asked the doctor about the long-term prognosis and he confirmed it was just a tiny vessel that had burst and that there shouldn't be any permanent damage.

When the tests were completed, Liora was put in a room on her own. This room had a smaller area attached to it that had a sink, some chairs and a large window that allowed you to sit in it and look into the main room.

By now it was mid-morning and our good friend Richard had brought Stuart to the hospital. Stuart had apparently slept in his clothes because he was in such a state. When he arrived, Stuart spoke to the neurologist himself. On hearing the good news, he was thankful that everything was going to be fine.

We arranged for our daughter Fiona to come to the hospital to see Liora. We were all so grateful after what had been such a terrible shock the night before. Judy stayed at home and looked after Adina and Miri.

My parents arrived from France that day. They had planned to spend the Passover holiday with us, although of course none of us expected that this was how we would be spending our time. Richard also collected my sister and niece from the airport. They had come over from France when they'd heard that Liora was not well.

Richard did a lot for us, driving people to and from the hospital. He had always been a great friend. When he was single, he would come to our house a lot for Friday night (Shabbat) dinner as he didn't have close family in London. He'd been like a big brother to the girls, helping the older ones learn to drive. He even let them sit in the driver's seat of his Aston Martin and pretend it was theirs.

Back at the house, Judy, our second eldest daughter, was looking after our relatives and cooking meals for everyone. It seemed as if all our friends and family were rallying round, helping us out in any way they could.

Back at the hospital, we had spent the day waiting for Liora to show signs of improvement. We'd been told she was going to recover, so now it was simply a matter of supporting her until she was better.

Then at about 4pm, everything suddenly changed. Liora's blood pressure suddenly shot up. We were told there was pressure on her brain. Apparently, she'd got an infection and the medical staff were finding it difficult to ventilate her and relieve the pressure in her chest.

They brought in portable machines to do a scan while Fiona, Stuart and I waited in the adjoining room. I was tapping and meditating trying to calm myself. Then a consultant asked to speak to Stuart and me alone.

That's when we were taken into the impersonal white room with the cold white tables and chairs. He said, 'I'm sorry to say that your daughter is seriously ill. There is swelling in her brain and she'll die tonight.'

If you've ever been told something that changes your life forever, you'll know how devastating this news was for us.

I came out of that room in a complete daze. Everything felt strange and surreal. My first reaction was to say, 'Well, that's what he said, there's nothing we can do.' I felt completely helpless.

Stuart told Fiona and Judy the bad news. But Fiona is also a qualified practitioner, so she can sense energy too. She said, 'No, she is alive, I can feel it. I know she's alive, she's moving a bit and I know she's alive.' Fiona then used the Theta Healing Muscle Test on me.

Muscle testing is a form of kinesiology that is used to identify beliefs that are held at the subconscious level. Fiona asked me a positive question around whether Liora was alive and my body moved forward, indicating an affirmative answer. It showed that subconsciously I sensed that Liora was alive.

When we were told the news that Liora was going to die, I texted Richard. My message was sent at 17:29 and it simply said: 'At her worst, bring the girls now, please.' Our youngest daughter, Miri, was having dinner with a friend when Richard collected her and her sisters. He drove so fast Miri was sick in his car.

Miri hadn't been inside a hospital since her birth, so the whole place felt very alien to her. She didn't want to go into Liora's room, so she just looked through the shutters from the adjoining room.

Miri started to feel sick again, so I had to take her out. We dashed into the first place we found, a small staff WC with a sink. An officious nurse came past and said, 'You can't be in there.' She was so insensitive. I was trying to cope with everyone else's feelings and reactions despite being terrified myself.

Miri was sick in the toilet and I was simultaneously sick in the sink.

I know some people will think I'm mad when I say this, but when I went back into Liora's room, I heard Liora talking. Through me, she announced: 'I am alive, I am alive.' I thought I was going crazy. How she could be talking to me?

Hesitantly, I said, 'I can hear her talking.' Fiona started asking me questions about characters in TV series and films. I hadn't seen them because they were programmes that only the girls watched. Answers from Liora started to come out of my mouth. The girls confirmed that the answers Liora was giving were correct. She even repeated a nickname she'd given Richard; a name I didn't know but which he confirmed was correct. Liora was channelling through me and that was what made me realise she was alive. It was then that I knew I needed to fight for her.

Prayers and support

Have you ever known you had to do something, even though it seemed crazy to everyone around you? When I realised that Liora was alive, I knew I had to be really determined and take action. I started to think about what I could do to help Liora and my first thought was to ask the community to say the Tehilim prayers (Psalms) for her.

On the first night, around 100 local people joined in the prayers and we noticed a slight improvement in Liora's condition. Even though the doctors had expected her to die that night, we saw her moving her leg and shoulder. There was hope.

Beyond the walls of the hospital, everyone in the community was very busy cleaning their houses, cooking special food or packing to go away for the Passover/Easter holiday. Despite this, they still took the time to pray for Liora.

My friend, Lauren Weinberg (whom I'd met when Liora modelled at a charity event) even invited people to her house to pray. This was despite the fact that she'd never said these specific prayers before.

After I told Lauren about Liora's improvement she decided to open a Facebook group. The group soon had over 15,000 people in it. They were from all over the world. They all prayed and offered to support Liora.

Over the next few days, we lived at the hospital, often eating and sleeping in the room next to Liora's. Food was sent to us by Jack Bendahan, the owner of the Kosher Deli. He labelled it for us and put it in a fridge in a designated room in the basement of the hospital. I knew Jack from when I used to collect leftovers from him to give to families in need. Liora had come with me to see him just a few weeks before. They had chatted easily and Liora had given him a blessing for donating the food. This was typical of Liora. She had always formed bonds with all sorts of people very easily.

As we sat watching over Liora, the machines continued to beep regularly. The nurses came in and out to record their observations and change the drips. But I was thinking about who could help us.

Throughout this time, our rabbi supported us enormously. He had helped me get some medical advice so I could understand a little more about what was going on. More advice was given by a rabbi who was also a retired doctor. He spoke to me on the phone, even though he was on holiday in Miami. When I told him what the readings on the machines said, he told me it didn't look good. But what I found out from him was that there are two ways a person can be declared dead; first, using a brain test and second, using a heart test.

Wednesday 20 April

On the morning of Wednesday 20 April, the hospital wanted to unplug Liora's life-support as they had expected her to die the night before. But we were determined that if she were to go, it would be at a time chosen by her, not them.

With Lauren Weinberg's help, we gathered together a legal team because we'd decided to appeal at court against having the machines turned off and her treatments discontinued. Liora looked so pale as she lay there with the tubes attached to her. Her amazing long brown hair framed her beautiful face.

The problem was that because Liora was 20, she was legally an adult, so we had no rights over what happened to her. Initially, I wasn't even allowed to see her medical file and we had to request it legally.

Stuart's brother, Jonathan, and Fiona looked after Liora so we could focus on the legal case and get a little sleep.

Stuart, Fiona and I had attended the first meeting with the medical staff, and it hadn't gone well. It was just us against a whole medical team. It was horrible and unpleasant.

When I explained to one of my holistic colleagues what had happened, she said, 'Why didn't you use your techniques?' Well, of course, I should have used them for the meeting, but I'd forgotten because I was so emotionally involved.

But at the next meeting, I used Colour Therapy to help the meeting go better. I visualised a shower of pink above the door of the room and clouds of gold around the medical team. The pink represented unconditional love while the gold was there to encourage more compassion and understanding. I worked on myself too. I used blue and pink, which are healing and loving colours.

As a result, the second meeting was much calmer and far more pleasant. We succeeded in getting the brain test postponed.

While we were at the hospital, we would sometimes be offered a room to sleep in. It was on the eleventh floor. We had to get the key from a security guard on the ground floor reception desk, signing for it at about 7pm and returning it before lunchtime the next day.

This should have been relatively simple, but during the Passover festival, there are certain restrictions that have to be observed. These restrictions include not using lifts and not writing. That meant that we were prevented from signing for the key ourselves and that we had to climb a lot of stairs. Because we were so tired and stressed, we found using the room physically demanding.

On Wednesday night I slept for the first time since the previous Sunday. Even though, on a normal day, I'd be tired by 11pm, I'd managed to keep going. It's amazing what the body can do in a crisis. If you've ever managed to keep going without getting proper rest because something important was going on in your life, you'll understand how I managed this.

Throughout this time, Liora continued to talk to me and once, when I was sleeping up on the eleventh floor, I heard her voice. It was about 4am and I heard her tell me that the drugs in her drip were running out. I rushed down to tell the nurse to put a new bag on – and this time, I used the lift rather than taking the stairs.

I barged into Liora's room, giving Jonathan and Fiona quite a fright because I was so loud and agitated. But I knew how desperately Liora needed the vitamins. The new bag was on the side desk and, fortunately, I'd managed to get there before the existing bag ran out.

Time passes

The days that followed were a bit of a blur. Liora's room had a window, so we could see when daylight turned to dusk and when darkness faded as the sun rose. Each day she was with us felt like a miracle.

As I held Liora's motionless hand, I kept saying: 'Don't go. Please stay…'. I told her how much I loved her and wanted her, and how much I needed her to stay. I knew it didn't matter what

I wanted, though. I knew that if she wanted to go, she would go and I had no control over the situation at all.

But it was important to me that *she* had that control, not the hospital. I wanted that for her.

I played her life over in my mind: her birth, moments from holidays, parties and just everyday life. I felt immense gratitude for each minute she stayed with me – not just the time in the hospital, but in her entire life. I was grateful for the joy she had brought me. I realised I was lucky to have known her at all.

The legal team fought hard to stop the life-support being turned off, while I and the rest of the family did energy work on Liora.

Fiona bathed her and washed her hair. We helped move her every three hours to stop her getting bedsores. Jonathan drove back and forth many times from Leeds to be with us and helped to bring other visitors to the hospital too. My sister-in-law Elissa and my nieces Jodie and Becky also came from Leeds to stay in London, so they could see Liora and support us. During the day, Judy sat at Liora's bedside while she read out a special prayer for those who are sick. In the evening, she went home to support her younger sisters.

It was hard because everyone wanted to be at the hospital with Liora, but they couldn't. We had to make sure that Adina and Miri felt loved and got the support they needed at this very difficult time.

Miri, in particular, found it difficult to come to the hospital. This was the first time she'd ever known anyone who was very ill, and this was her dear sister, so it was a traumatic experience for her. As the hospital scared her so much, Miri only visited Liora there once. This visit affected her deeply and for a time she found it difficult even to say the word 'hospital'. Later, I did some energy work with her so she could say the word without feeling afraid.

Stuart, Judy, Fiona, Adina, our Rabbi and I also prayed a lot at Liora's bedside. Hershel Grunfeld and the patient liaison and advocacy service were very helpful too.

I asked the nurses who came in the room to talk to Liora and explain what they were doing. I wanted the staff to understand that Liora could hear everything, even though she could not move. I wanted them to treat her like a human being.

We made sure Liora had meditations and positive affirmations to listen to (see page 85). We also played music and Louise Hay readings such as 'You Can Heal Your Life' and morning and evening meditations. Initially I put headphones on Liora, but they wouldn't stay on, so I just let everything play out loud. This was good for everyone as it meant the staff as well as the family could gain from them, as well as Liora.

There were lots of visitors. Rachel Posner, a friend, came to the hospital with Lauren Weinberg. They were very helpful and supportive for the girls. A young man called Aaron sent me a message asking if he could come in to sing and play the guitar for Liora. I said yes, even though I didn't know him. But when he arrived, to my surprise, I realised that I knew his mum, Nicole, and that his brother Sam was one of Liora's best friends.

I'd met Nicole one day when I'd gone to feed Liora in the Mother and Baby room at Boots. She had been there too with Sam. After that we arranged play dates for the children. Liora and Sam were in the same class at primary school, too. Unfortunately, I hadn't seen Nicole for a while, so it was good to make the connection again even in these difficult circumstances.

The story behind Aaron coming in is quite amazing. He had been trying to organise times to go and play music for the elderly, but none of the organisations he'd contacted had called him back. Later, he told me that he'd felt really disappointed and rather rejected about it. But with hindsight, he believed there was a reason why nobody had returned his calls, and that was because he was meant to play for Liora instead.

Each day we read messages of support on the Facebook group and about all the amazing things people were doing around the world to support us. It really helped. Friends were also taking cooked food to my home for my parents and the girls. Sylvie Leboulanger, a cranial osteopath, also came to work on Liora at the hospital.

At one meeting with the consultant, I managed to convince them to allow us to bring in Liora's dog, Whisky. I was hoping it would help her wake up.

Adina was responsible for bringing Whisky to hospital; she prepared him for the journey, kept him calm in the car and brought with her everything he needed for the visit. Even though she was only 13 at the time, she behaved with great maturity and I was immensely grateful for her help and initiative.

When Whisky arrived at the hospital, it took him a long time to settle on Liora's bed. He licked her hand, but she hardly responded.

Throughout this time, I sent and received emails and was on the phone constantly getting advice from various rabbis, the legal team, my colleagues and friends about Liora's condition. I did this from within Liora's room in Intensive Care. We never left Liora alone. My husband is a solicitor, so he was also checking all the documents.

We believed that some of Liora's functions had shut down, so she had more energy to allow her body to heal. Given time, we believed she could recover. We found some research showing that Vitamin C could help stimulate brain cell growth. Ilan Slazenger got in touch with me through Facebook and sent me lots of documentation and studies about Vitamin C and was even prepared to supply the products himself.

Judy put it all together at home and made up a file, so we had something to show the consultant. I managed to get Ilan to discuss it on the phone with him, but unfortunately, he wasn't prepared to try the treatment. The consultant emailed us to say that there was 'no solid scientific evidence that this is a safe, effective, and appropriate treatment for this case, and that means that our hands are tied, unfortunately.'

At one point during this time, I heard that one of my daughters had said to my brother-in-law, 'Now I know why you can't open the windows in hospitals.' She'd felt extremely low on seeing the plight of her sister. I had been looking everywhere for her and eventually found her upset in the toilet.

Liora with Whisky, our dog

At the same time, Adina was looking after our house and two dogs at just 13 years old. She even had to run after one of them when someone left the front door open. From the day Liora went into hospital, she became an adult, taking on a lot of responsibility.

Eight days after we had managed to get the brain test postponed, we lost the case. We were in a room with our lawyers when the doctors told us the court judgement. Within 10 minutes of that meeting, they wanted to do the brain test. Fiona rang me on my mobile panicking, telling me they were in the room. I ran into the room screaming, but I couldn't stop them.

I completely lost my temper. I shouted, banged on the doors and went completely mad, but they said, 'No, we are still doing it, there's nothing that can stop us now.'

The solicitor said we could appeal, but if we lost then they would unplug her life-support on Friday morning. Our rabbi advised us to try to negotiate with the hospital to give Liora a bit more time.

That afternoon they did the test and to our horror, they did it in front of us. The whole test was very mechanical. It felt heartless and was awful to witness. Liora didn't respond.

I didn't want her to be unplugged; I wanted her to die naturally and in her own time. Following a consultation with a group of rabbis, an agreement was reached with the medical team that they would simply allow the blood pressure drug to run out.

After that point, and for the last two days, whenever I heard Liora's voice it was faint. I realised that she wasn't quite there anymore, so I knew something was different. On the last day, I could hardly hear her anymore. I knew she was getting weak. I thought she might not be able to fight the lung infection.

The blood pressure medication ran out around 4pm on Saturday afternoon. The medical team thought she would go within 10 minutes. A nurse who was pregnant with her first child was left on watch in the room, but she found it extremely hard to watch and had to keep leaving the room because she was upset. Eventually she was replaced by another nurse.

All we wanted at this point was an extra four hours so we could get past 9pm and finish Shabbat. We didn't want the festival of Passover to be marred forever by the anniversary of Liora's passing.

I posted this message on the Facebook group: 'Please, please, Liora is still on the life-support machine, but they stopped her noradrenalin, so her blood pressure is dropping fast. She needs all of you to send her your love and healing right now, please. Thank you.'

I was hoping Liora would last until at least Sunday, but I was worried they would not give us that long. They could have come in at any time and changed their mind about letting her go naturally.

With our help and Liora's own will, she managed to last a few extra hours, which meant we would not always have the anniversary of her death on the festival of Passover. This was important because it had always been her favourite festival.

We searched the internet for techniques that would raise blood pressure by using pressure points. The information wasn't easy to find though as most sites focused on how to lower blood pressure rather than raise it.

The minute the drug ran out, Liora's heart rate crashed and her blood pressure started to plummet. We frantically worked on her pressure points to raise her blood pressure. Stuart was doing the pressure points on one of Liora's hands, Judy on the other and Fiona was working on her feet. I adjusted the bed so that Liora's head was lower than her feet. She was still being fed through the tubes, so I had to be extremely careful not to damage any of them. We covered her with heated blankets to maintain her temperature, which had dropped to 34°C.

We were working on Liora frantically. We never thought we would have to use the machines, so we weren't sure how to use them, even though we'd watched the staff using them for days. The monitors bleeped and pinged, sending out seemingly indecipherable information intended only for those with medical knowledge, of which we had none.

The nurse had been told not to do anything, so it was down to us. We were doing everything. For the next few hours, we worked on Liora. I did all the energy healing I could, following guidance that my colleagues Ilka Wandel and Toks Coker gave me over the phone. As a result, Liora's blood pressure went up and we managed to stabilise it. But it was gradually going down.

We kept a constant check on the numbers displayed on the monitors. I couldn't see the screens very well from the position I was in, so Judy was telling me the numbers. Squatting and squashed between the machines, I was on the phone for six hours getting instructions.

I felt so sorry that our daughters had to go through this. I wouldn't wish it on anyone; to be in hospital and have to work on your own sister to try to save her. We knew she needed more time to heal, but unfortunately the medical system did not give us that time. Although brain cells do reproduce, it takes a long time and we didn't have that time.

We anxiously worked on Liora until, at 9.26pm, all the numbers went down to zero. She had lived an extra 12 days because we had battled to keep her alive with the help of the Creator. She had gone when she wanted to go and it was after the Shabbat.

When all the machines showed a flat line and no heart rate, Judy screamed so loud that I think Fiona and I will always remember it. It was such a cry of desperation, loss and sadness.

That night Rabbi Ginsbury and his wife came to the hospital to support us, along with our friends Jack and Carole-Ann Bendahan, and Jonathan and Richard. Richard was unable to come up and see us as in the Jewish religion he is a Cohen and a Cohen is not allowed to be near the dead.

I wanted to go home to tell Miri, Adina and my parents that Liora had passed away, but I needed to be at the hospital. I was desperate that Miri and Adina didn't find out from someone else, so I called Chagit and asked her to go to our house and tell

When the Unthinkable Happened

my parents. I wanted to hold Adina and Miri in my arms so tight, but I couldn't be in two places at once.

Stuart and Jonathan stayed with Liora's body all night to ensure that Jewish traditions could be upheld. Even though it was a Bank Holiday weekend, people were incredibly kind. There was even a waiting list of those offering to sit with Liora's body until the funeral.

The Rabbi and his wife eventually drove Judy, Fiona and I home at 4am. We were completely broken. It was the quietest and saddest journey I have ever made.

In the next section of the book, I'll show you some of the techniques and thought processes that helped my family and me move forward and cope following Liora's passing.

But before I do that, I'd like to share the readings from Liora's funeral and stone-setting ceremony as well as some words about our journey in life. I hope that you, like me, will find these both moving and motivating.

Love, Light and Liora

24 FEATURE · THE JEWISH WEEKLY · 13 SEPTEMBER 2018

LIFE WITHOUT LIORA

Lauren Rosenberg speaks to Lara Rosenfelder about how she deals with her daughter's death

Lauren has become even more acutely aware of the need to be grateful for all that is good in her life

Newspaper article about life without Liora

32

CHAPTER 2
THE FUNERAL

Funeral, Wednesday 4 May 2016

Liora's funeral took place on Wednesday 4 May 2016 and was led by Rabbi Mordechai Ginsbury of Hendon United Synagogue. This is his address.

'Lauren, Stuart, Judy, Fiona, Adina and Miri – from the very first moment we saw one another, after dear Liora was stricken with the terrible brain haemorrhage which was to take her away from you and all of us, we committed 'to leave no stone unturned' in yearning, striving for and believing in a 'miracle of miracles' which would yet keep her here with us. So very sadly, it was not to be, all your and our herculean efforts notwithstanding.

Liora was so talented and blessed with special gifts which she used to such good effect throughout her all too short life – her smile that would light up a room, her prodigious artistic ability, being awarded the very top prize for art as she concluded her A-Level in that subject at JFS; her warm and enthusiastic personality which made her such a natural and popular teaching assistant, and, above all, such a greatly loved daughter, sister, granddaughter and good and loyal friend to many. The world will be the poorer without her positivity and her own holistic healing talents, skills she shared, in common with her dear mother. Lauren, Stuart and family – we, and so very many others, have been through so much together these past few days and weeks, it is difficult, if not impossible, to know where to start, where to finish...

Just one theme I would share with you once again, which I believe has been a sustaining one for you, first and foremost, but for all of us as well – through this so very painful and tragic episode. There were many small, but highly significant miracles and moments of light throughout the terrible darkness of Liora's short but remorseless indisposition.

The thousands and thousands of people across the globe who rallied to Liora's support, responding to what was, initially, a small group of close family and friends marshalling good deeds that Liora might merit, which mushroomed into a huge social media support group, giving tremendous support and encouragement to Liora's family. There were also many hundreds of people who gathered together, almost without any notice, at readings, to pray for Liora's recovery. The huge amount of money raised, which accrues to Liora's merit, and those times when you so much needed a particular friend, family member, advisor and/or helper to 'be there' for/with you ... and they were just there. (And if I do mention just one person by name, it probably has to be Stuart's dear brother, Jonathan, who spent so much time with you at Liora's bedside and did so much to be there with, and for, you.) The remarkable response by so many, who gave up their time at all hours of the day and night to sit with Liora, so that Liora was not left alone for a moment, from the time of her passing until this funeral service. All signs, that even in your pretty much unbearable grief and anguish, you are not alone.

Rather than say any more words of my own at this point, I am just going to read out two messages, almost verbatim, amongst the very many which Lauren and Stuart have received since Liora's passing, and which they have requested I share with everyone here today. The first is from someone who has only just come to know Liora and her family through the recent tragedy; the second is from an old family friend.'

Message from a new friend

'I was thinking about the name Liora, and its meaning in Hebrew. Li-Ora, the first thought is that it means: my light. But that's not completely right, the word "li" in Hebrew doesn't mean "my" or "mine" but rather "to me" or "for me", thus "light for me".

And yet, there's more to it, because if you look deeper, "ora" is not just a simple light but a bigger one, a big light that brings redemption and happiness to all who see it.

That's what Liora did the past two weeks – she brought a big light to the world, a light that brought redemption and happiness to numerous people around the globe, me amongst them. So, thank you, Liora, for letting me be involved in your story, and thank you, Rosenberg family, for introducing me to her most beautiful, redeeming, full-of-happiness light.'

Message from an old family friend

'Dear Lauren, I have been trying to find the words all day to drop you a note. Fighting back the tears I have shed since I read your posting this morning, I am still not managing.

I remember Liora as a beautiful baby. I recollect coming to your home for Friday night dinner, a few months after Liora was born. I was in awe of such a beautiful baby, maybe it's because you were the first of my friends to have children, or, as I now know, there was something special about Liora – something which could light up a room and people's hearts.

I know we have not seen each other as often as we did; however, our families have always had a connection. As you will remember, Stuart was a neighbour from Leeds and of course we have known each other from our single days, which is longer than either of us care to remember!

In Memory of a wonderful
Daughter

We'll never see your face again
or hear your gentle voice
we had to let you go
for we had no other choice
We've searched our hearts for answers
and asked endless questions why
yet still we cannot understand
no matter how we try
In life you were loved dearly
in death we love you still -
there'll always be a place in our hearts
that only you can fill

Anonymous

The way you have conducted yourself over the past two weeks has been beyond admirable – every time I have looked at Facebook the first thing I looked for was your updates – hoping and praying there would be some better news.

Today's outcome is the one we all prayed would not happen. However, I hope that you will take comfort knowing that you did everything you could (and more) for your darling Liora. Liora has united a community – and not just a Jewish one – in a way that probably nobody else could do in a whole lifetime. It has made everyone who heard her story re-evaluate their life and see how they can improve themselves and their world.

I cannot imagine the immense pain caused by your loss, the loss that no parent should ever suffer. Please take comfort in that what Liora has done for our community. I wish you, Stuart, Judy, Fiona, Adina and Miri a long life and only happy memories of your darling Liora.'

'Liora – what can we say to you at this most difficult moment? You have clearly always had a quiet but so very meaningful influence on those who've had the pleasure of knowing and being close to you. In your passing, you have elicited positivity and goodness on an extraordinary scale from many thousands of people around the world. Your last day on Earth was the 8th day of Pesach and you passed away as we counted the 8th day of the Omer. Eight in Jewish tradition represents an elevation from the ordinary to the extraordinary, the natural to the supernatural.

Claim your due recompense and deserved place of honour in the hereafter. Please ask for mercy – for your grief-stricken parents, sisters, family and many friends. We ask your forgiveness and indulgence – if there was something we could have done but didn't do for you, and pray that your dear and precious soul should be bound up in the bond of eternal life, and your resting place should be one of only deserved honour and glory.'

Stone-Setting Ceremony

Liora's memorial stone

Liora's Stone-Setting Ceremony took place on Sunday 19 March 2017. It was a wet day. This is Fiona's speech:

'I am not one to speak about how I feel, especially not in public, but I wanted to express to you today how I saw my big sister, Liora.

Twenty years isn't a lot, but I will never forget the 17 years that we had together. Whether it was singing in the car at the top of our voices, doing each other's make-up, or simply having a coffee together – our relationship wasn't like most siblings, it was much more. Most of you who know us five girls will know that we have always been very close.

The night that we lost Liora, I didn't just lose my sister, I lost my best friend, my role model – my everything. Liora and I had made so many plans for the future, and I will do my best to carry them out. I hope one day she will look down from Shamayim [Heaven] and be proud of me.

Liora accomplished so much, and if there's one thing we can take from her short life, it is to live every day to its fullest potential, and not to take anything for granted.

Life is a journey, and you don't know where it will take you. However, we all have a choice – we can choose to sit along for the ride or take every opportunity that is thrown at us, and live life to the full – and that is exactly what Liora did.

Liora was one of the most kind and caring people I knew. If you ever needed her, she would always be there for you with a smile on her face and wouldn't leave without you having a smile on your face. Her smile was contagious, and her love for life was infectious.

Liora fulfilled so much in her 20 years, winning the art award at JFS, becoming the youngest holistic practitioner in the UK, writing her own book and running an art camp – and we sisters couldn't be prouder. I hope one day I will be a quarter of the person that she was. If I hadn't had Liora as my sister, I would not be the person I am today.

We are told so often that everything happens for a reason, but when you lose a sister, a daughter, a granddaughter, it leaves a massive void and many unanswered questions. I sincerely hope that with time, we may understand the ways of Hashem. We may have lost Liora, but Hashem has gained a gorgeous and precious angel. Thank you.'

There was an amazing point during the stone-setting ceremony when the rain suddenly stopped, and the sun lit up Liora's name on the stone – it was beautiful and so typically Liora. Many people commented on this moment.

Something else that took my breath away happened on my birthday a few months later. I looked up and saw a flock of birds flying in this formation. It made me think of Liora because, to me, the shape the birds made looked like an 'L'.

Birds flying as a letter 'L'

Our Train Journey

'At birth we board the train and meet our parents, and we believe they will always travel by our side. However, at one stop, our parents will step down from the train, leaving us on this journey alone.

As time goes by, other people will board the train; and they will be significant, i.e. our siblings, friends, children, and even the love of our life. Many will step down and leave a permanent vacuum. Others will go so unnoticed that we don't realize that they vacated their seats. This train ride will be full of joy, sorrow, fantasy, expectations, hellos, goodbyes, and farewells. Success consists of having a good relationship with all passengers, requiring that we give the best of ourselves.

The mystery to everyone is: we do not know at which station we ourselves will step down. So, we must live in the best way, love, forgive, and offer the best of who we are. It is important to do this because when the time comes for us to step down, and leave our seat empty, we should leave behind beautiful memories for those who will continue to travel on the train of life. I wish you a joyful journey.'

(Author Unknown)

In *Memory* of a

Loved One

You're in every gentle raindrop
and EACH glint of *morning* dew
you're the breeze that softly WHISPERS
and the autumn's *golden* hue

You're in winter's GENTLE snowfalls
and the warming *summer* sun
and the FIRST bright, fragrant flowers
when the springtime's just *begun*

For although I really MISS you
always have and *always* will
nature's BEAUTY all around me
lets me know you're with me *still*

You were *loved* so much in LIFE
and now that you are gone
I'll LOOK for you in life's *best* things
and in them, you'll live on

Anonymous

CHAPTER 3
DEALING WITH GRIEF AND LOSS

People deal with grief in different ways. In 1969, Kubler-Ross identified that people generally go through five stages when dealing with grief:

- Denial

- Anger

- Bargaining

- Depression

- Acceptance

This process is often represented as a curve and different people take different amounts of time to go through each of the stages. However, grieving isn't a process that's confined to death (mourning); other life events can lead to a period of grieving, such as divorce, job loss, illness and changes in the family, such as children growing up or relatives moving away.

What to say to someone who's grieving
Despite grief being such a common experience, people rarely know how to relate to someone who's mourning.

Indeed, one of the many issues I've had to deal with since Liora passed is that people seem to struggle to know what to say to us. Some have ignored me, others have tried to avoid me, and some seem totally tongue-tied and awkward or say the wrong thing.

What I want (and what most people who've lost someone want) is for people to simply treat them normally. Talk about the same things you've always talked about because even though something tragic has happened, we are all still the same people.

I may have lost Liora, but I still want to be asked about the rest of my family and what's going on in my life. And, of course, I want to share their news too. I hope they will talk to me about Liora and the wonderful things she did when she was with us. The anonymous quote below sums up my own thoughts. I also found it frustrating that people who said they'd visit or provide support didn't follow through. I wish they hadn't said those things if they didn't mean them. But, I'm very grateful for the people who've stayed in our lives and continue to help us.

The ideas listed on page 46 come from Marie Forleo's YouTube video called 'What To Say (And Not To Say) When Someone Dies or Suffers a Tragedy'.

If you know someone who has lost a very important person in their life and you're afraid to mention them because you think you may make them sad by reminding them that they died—you're not reminding them, they didn't forget that they died. What you're reminding them of is that you remembered that they lived. And that is a great, great gift.

Sharing grief

I know that for many, death and grief are taboo subjects. But all of us will experience loss at some point so I want to encourage you to share your grief. If we share our vulnerability with others, we can create much closer bonds.

It's easy to feel that you should shut yourself off when you're struggling with grief, but I believe it's better to reach out to those you trust at difficult times. They may have ideas and insights that might help us, and they can also give us the nurturing care we need. It's when we're in need that we discover who's willing to walk alongside us. After all, we would help them in the same way. Sometimes it's the people we least expect who give us the most support. But if we don't open up, we'll never find out. Along with our own strength and resilience, letting others in can help us manage the burden of grief.

We can also check our thoughts and feelings by talking to others. Understanding our feelings can help release us from the guilt or the selfishness we might have about sharing our grief.

Sharing in this way can also help others have a greater understanding of their own feelings and help them become more empathetic. When we share our fears, pain, joy and hopes, we share the universe's wisdom and its loving care.

Don't	Do
Say 'I know exactly how you feel'.	Reach out and offer a shoulder to lean on.
Push your opinions.	Keep checking in.
Share that you knew someone with the same problem or issue, and it didn't turn out well.	Say 'I'm so sorry'.
Start with the words 'At least'.	Say 'I wish I had the right words; just know I care'.
Say 'It's just stuff,' or 'It's just money,' or 'It's just anything'.	Say 'I'm always just a phone call away'.
Make it a discussion of God, faith or religion.	Say 'How can I help you'.
Say 'They're in a better place'.	Offer to help in specific ways.
Say 'There's a reason for everything'.	Tell stories and share memories about the person.
Say 'It was her time to go'.	Send a card in the post.
Say 'She was such a good person, God wanted her to be with Him'.	Keep in contact during the year and after.
Say 'Be strong'.	Be yourself.

Tapping

Tapping (or Emotional Freedom Technique) is one technique you can use to help with grief. You can use it to eliminate unresolved negative emotions caused by loss so you can move forward. It's described in detail in Chapter 7. Other techniques you can use include essential oils, colour therapy, music and visualisations, but there are many more.

Choosing What to Believe About Death

It's up to you to choose what to believe about death because you decide what you think and how you feel. Different religions have varying beliefs. When I read the following words from the writings of Paramahansa Yogananda, I found them very comforting.

'Though the ordinary man looks upon death with dread and sadness, those who have gone before know it as a wondrous experience of peace and freedom.

At death, you forget all the limitations of the physical body and realise how free you are. For the first few seconds there is a sense of fear – fear of the unknown, of something unfamiliar to the consciousness. But after that comes a great realisation: the soul feels a joyous sense of relief and freedom. You know that you exist from the mortal body.

Every one of us is going to die someday, so there is no use in being afraid of death. You don't feel miserable at the prospect of losing consciousness of your body in sleep; you accept sleep as a state of freedom to look forward to. So is death; it is a state of rest, a suspension from life. There is nothing to fear. When death comes, laugh at it. Death is only an experience through which you are meant to learn a great lesson: you cannot die.

Our real self, the soul, is immortal. We may sleep for a little while in that change called death, but we can never be destroyed. We exist, and existence is eternal. The wave comes to the shore, and then goes back to the sea; it is not lost. It becomes one with the ocean or returns again in the form of another wave. This body has come, and it will vanish;

but the soul essence within it will never cease to exist. Nothing can terminate that eternal consciousness.

Even a particle of matter or a wave of energy is indestructible, as science has proved; the soul of spiritual essence of man is also indestructible. Matter undergoes change; the soul undergoes changing experiences. Radical changes are termed death, but death or a change in form does not change or destroy the spiritual essence.

The body is only a garment. How many times you have changed your clothing in this life, yet because of this you would not say that you have changed. Similarly, when you give up this bodily dress at death you do not change. You are just the same, an immortal soul, a child of God.'

I've heard death referred to as 'emigrating to heaven'. After my experience, this is how I see death now. I think we are born into a body and leave it when we 'die'; we still exist, just in a different form. An important point to remember is that the love you have for the person who has passed away will always be with you because love never dies.

I don't like the expression 'I am sorry for your loss' as I don't feel I have lost my daughter. I may have lost the physical part of her, but she is still very much with us. Energy never dies.

Liora and our neighbour Lou, celebrating Lou's 100th birthday

PART 2:
LIGHT

CHAPTER 4
FOCUS ON POSITIVE THOUGHTS

After a traumatic event or major unwanted change in our lives, many of us have negative thoughts and unwelcome feelings that we need to manage. These thoughts and feelings could include anger, resentment, despair and sadness. These are emotions that are hard to deal with.

What's worse is that we can also feel stuck because we're not sure how to cope and how to move beyond these difficult times.

The problem is that if these feelings aren't managed well from the start, a difficult but temporary situation can last for years, and for some even a lifetime. It's easy to forget how to be happy because life becomes so bleak.

Negative thoughts and feelings like anger and hatred hold you back and block your energy, causing both physical and emotional trauma. To release this negativity, you need to turn your anger into love, and shift your expectations and beliefs so that you focus on positive thoughts and feelings. This way, you'll attract more of what you want into your life.

Quantum Physics has revealed that the universe is made up purely of energy; everything is energy. It's an amazing idea. But what it means is that as well as everything else in our world, our thoughts are also energy, which means they can change what we perceive and experience, making the world a reflection of our own beliefs and expectations.

When we focus on our negative thoughts and emotions, we create a negative world around us. Just as a magician diverts our attention so we can't see how he does his tricks, so our negative thoughts distract us from the good things in life and make us unhappy. It can often seem as the negative world is the real world, but that isn't the case.

You have the capacity to be happy and fulfilled. I believe you are unique and were born to stand out and lead a life of joy; I hope you believe this too and want to create a life you love.

You can do this, but only if you don't allow yourself to get into a low mood. That will only lead to depression.

When you get into a negative state of mind, the only certainty is that you won't experience the amazing opportunities that life has to offer. In fact, your negative thoughts will leave you feeling trapped and purposeless. You'll literally feel dragged down by your problems because that's all you'll be able to see.

So, in order to move from a low mood to one of joy, you first need to understand where you are emotionally.

To get started, take a moment to observe how you're feeling right now. Think about lots of different adjectives that describe emotions.

Using the space provided on the next page or your own journal or notebook, answer the questions that follow.

This will help you start to get a clearer picture of your current emotional state. It will also help you to start thinking about what you would like to achieve going forward.

Write your answers to the questions in the spaces below.

1: What words would you use to describe the way you feel right now?

....

....

2: Are you content with your life? If not, why not?

....

....

3: Would you choose to feel the way you do? Why?

....

4: List three goals you still want to achieve in your life:

i) ....

ii) ....

iii) ....

5: If you died tomorrow, who would attend your funeral?

....

....

6: What words would the mourners use to describe you?

....

....

7: Would you be leaving behind an inspiring legacy?

....

....

We'll look at your answers later, but first, let me tell you about the legacy Liora left, as I hope it'll inspire you to think differently about yourself.

Liora's legacy

Liora was a miracle in herself. When I got married, my gynaecologist told me I probably wouldn't get pregnant for at least four years. In fact, I fell pregnant with Liora very soon after getting married! I was married in March 1995 and Liora was born in January 1996.

Many people have told me how impressed they were not only by how much Liora achieved during her lifetime but also by the impact she had on many people during her short time on earth. I believe she continues to have a lasting influence. Many people said she achieved more in her 20 years than many people do in 80 or more. Sometimes it's hard to comprehend the impact she had, and still has. In some ways, she was just an ordinary girl, but in many ways, she was wise beyond her years.

Liora has left a huge legacy. For a start, she always had a smile on her face, she made connections with everyone she met, and she was willing to work hard to achieve her goals.

For example, she won an art award in school despite being told she wasn't good at art (see next page). She wasn't a natural artist, but she worked at it until she was good at it. That's a reminder to all of us to be willing to work hard to achieve our dreams.

An art prize for Year 10 pupils has now been set up at her school in her honour, and we recently displayed her artwork in an exhibition. One day, I'd love there to be a specific Art Day in secondary schools across the UK on her birthday (12 January).

Liora collecting her art award at JFS

I believe that schools focus too much on academic work and try to mould all children to be the same and forget that we are all 'unique'. More time needs to be spent on creative activities, allowing children to express themselves and celebrate their individuality. Many studies show that art can also have a healing effect.

To see this painting finished, turn to page 66

As well as being a happy, warm person who worked hard at the things that were important to her, Liora was also a qualified therapist. She trained in a range of disciplines including: Modern Energy Techniques (at just 16 years of age), Emo Trance, Integral Eye Movement Therapy, Theta Healing and Positive Tapping. She attended many training sessions with me and passed all the tests. She was also learning Picture Tapping.

She created products to help others, writing a '21-day Positive Mindset' programme and publishing the '365 Affirmations for Teens Calendar'. When she died, she was in the middle of designing several other self-help programmes and a piece of art entitled 'Happiness is Made from Home'. You can read the goals she wrote in her notebook on the next page.

She aspired to:

- Be a recognised artist.

- Have a modelling career and be as successful as Cara Delevingne by 2017.

- Get married.

- Have enough money to be financially free.

- Have a programme in place to help teenagers.

She also reminded herself in these notes to 'focus on the positive' and remember Esther Hicks' Law of Attraction.

As well as working on her own projects, Liora was always pushing me to complete my own. She was helping me to write a new therapy manual. With her encouragement, I also designed my 'Happy Child Affirmations Calendar'. The Facebook group that was set up when Liora was in hospital had over 15,000 members. The group is called 'Do a Mitzvah in the name of Liora Rosenberg'. Mitzvah is a Hebrew word meaning 'good deed'.

People sometimes accuse social media users of being insecure and using it to brag or moan, but we received an amazing heartfelt response to Liora's sudden illness.

I'm still in awe when I look back at some of the posts now; there were children writing Liora's name in the sand on the beach when they were on their foreign holidays, someone having her long, dark hair (which was just like Liora's) cut off and given to charity, and another teenager giving blood. Even soldiers in the Israeli army prayed for her.

We gave out this card at Liora's school (JFS)

Even though people didn't know Liora, they still wanted to do something to support her and our family. It didn't seem to matter where they lived or what religion they followed – they just wanted to do something positive to help. It gave me, my husband and our girls strength to know that people cared so much.

The Facebook group that was created when Liora was ill is full of love and unity. It's amazing! Maybe that's one of the reasons Liora was born: to unite people with unconditional love and to spread unconditional love. (You can see some of the many posts from the Facebook group at the end of this book in Chapter 10).

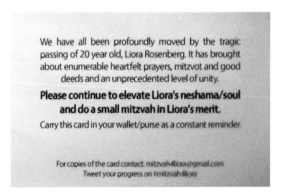

The reverse side of the card given out at Liora's school (JFS)

Only days before she became ill, Liora and I had been chatting about what we would do if we won the lottery. Liora said that she would buy an ambulance for Hatzola (the medical emergency response service). So, when she was ill in hospital, we set up a fundraising campaign to do just that.

The activities we used to raise money included: cake sales (my daughters Judy and Fiona love to bake), selling sweets (Miri raised £35), asking friends for donations (Adina raised £150), and we've held two concerts. We have had amazing support.

At the concerts, several of the performers said they felt Liora's presence and light. There were some great singers including Sada Vidoo, who'd been on *The X Factor*, and Liora's best friend Charlotte. She performed a song she had written about Liora.

Sam Shaker, the owner of the club, Jazz After Dark in Soho, London, also presented us with a portrait he'd painted of Liora, which was really special. He is an artist and was also very close to Amy Winehouse.

Sam Shaker's portrait of Liora

Liora truly loved to give to others. She helped me with collections of food for those in need and had modelled for charity.

I also remember a time when Liora invited a friend of my youngest daughter to have a sleepover with her because she sensed this little girl needed some extra attention. The seven-year-old was completely thrilled to be with Liora.

Liora also said she wanted to set up a charity that would send flowers to those who were going through tough times. While developing her artistic career, Liora was also working as a teaching assistant. On her way home from work, she walked past a florist called Blue Valley. She'd mentioned to me that she wished she had the courage to go into the shop and ask the owner whether he would be able to donate unused flowers to her charity.

After she died, I told Daniel Tendler (the then manager of Blue Valley) what had happened to Liora and about her wish to send flowers. He agreed to help, so we started Liora's Flower Gemach (meaning 'acts of kindness') locally. Now, a number of people help by donating flowers. I'd love to expand it nationwide, perhaps with the help of a major supermarket.

This is the logo for Liora's Flower Gemach

Giving flowers helps in so many ways. It's not just the beauty of them with their many colours, but also the scent. Flowers ignite the senses. People who have received flowers through Liora's charity have very much appreciated the fact that someone cares about them. They also say they enjoy having someone to talk to, even if it's only briefly, as it helps them feel less isolated. In turn, my family and I have found that helping others also helps us cope with missing Liora.

Some people have found it difficult to speak to me since her passing. I think this is typical; people feel, 'I don't know what to say,' and 'I don't want to say the wrong thing.' I understand these thoughts and feelings, but please don't avoid me, don't turn away; acknowledge Liora and her gifts. Talk to me about what she did, who she was and how she had an impact on you; let's celebrate and acknowledge that.

If you are struggling to cope with the loss of a loved one or to find the right words to say to someone who is grieving, please take a look at some of the wording on page 46. I have found them useful and they might help you too.

I'm pleased to say that many people do speak to me and message me, so I see the impact this tragic event has had on others. Some are now living more loving and compassionate lives as a result of what happened to Liora.

For me, the impact that this unthinkable event has had is to make me realise that I must share my experience and what I have learned from it. I would like to help you. I want my impact to be positive, to add value to your life and to know that I didn't waste what I was given. I want to know that Liora didn't pass away for nothing. I want to help you turn things around, make a difference and have a greater impact yourself.

I've heard a phrase recently, 'Don't be bitter, be better.'

I like it because it encourages us to use our experiences to move forward rather than staying stuck in a place of rage and resentment.

Liora modelling at a charity event

So, the next time you take your child to school, think of the privilege you enjoy in being able to do that simple task.

I can no longer take Liora out or drive with her somewhere. See the positive in everything and enjoy all your moments with your children.

If you found the earlier exercise around thinking about your funeral a bit depressing, why not look just a few months ahead instead? Build a little more on the answers you wrote on page 55.

Describe the feelings you would like to experience more of:

....

....

....

....

Of the three goals you wrote down earlier, which do you *most* want to achieve?

....

....

....

....

What words would you like others to use to describe you?

....

....

....

When people hear you're going to be at a meeting or social gathering, what do you want them to be thinking or saying? 'Oh great, he/she always has lots of interesting/funny/useful things to say' or 'I always enjoy seeing him/her' or 'I feel really upbeat after chatting with him/her.'

After all, that's far better than, 'Oh no, is he/she really coming? He/she is always miserable and full of doom and gloom' or 'It's a real effort to have a conversation with him/her, and I always feel dragged down afterwards.'

Now that you know of some of the fabulous things Liora achieved in her lifetime, start to think about what you want to achieve in your own life. How do you want others to talk about you? What would you love to hear them saying about you?

This is the finished painting Liora was creating on page 58

CHAPTER 5
THE POWER OF A POSITIVE MINDSET

I took the photo below at the clinic where two of our daughters went for grief counselling. I like it because it sums up the way I think and want to lead my life.

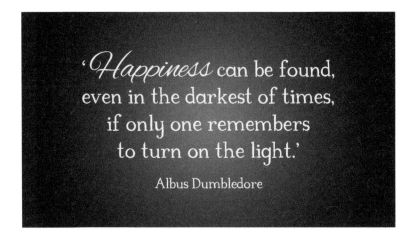

'*Happiness* can be found, even in the darkest of times, if only one remembers to turn on the light.'

Albus Dumbledore

These words were spoken by Cassidy Stay, from Texas, USA, during the memorial for her family when her mother, father and four younger siblings were killed during a terrible gun attack in 2014. She was just 15 at the time.

The line was originally spoken by Harry Potter's mentor Dumbledore, who is played by Sir Michael Gambon in the Harry Potter films. The character says it as he addresses the pupils of Hogwarts in the Great Hall at the start of *The Prisoner of Azkaban*. Liora didn't enjoy the Harry Potter films, but despite this, the quote still resonates with me. Maybe it's because the word 'light' is part of the meaning of Liora's name.

I also think of light in the sense of 'getting lighter'. We feel lighter when we move forward from being stuck and find the solutions for our problems. Spreading love and light is one of the key aspects I want to get across in this book.

Liora's passing, like that of the Stay family, is tragic, but I don't think that means we can't be happy. I've heard people who've experienced something terrible say, 'I don't think I'll ever be happy again' and while I can understand their feelings, I also believe that if we never experienced happiness after a painful experience, we would all be wasting our lives.

I know Liora understands that if we smile, laugh and experience joy, it doesn't mean that we loved her less. Indeed, it's often when looking at pictures and remembering things she did that I smile the most.

It's worth noticing though, that the quote says: 'If one only *remembers* to turn on the light'. To me, this acknowledges that we must be open to letting the light in and that sometimes we might need to take action to allow this to happen.

Liora wrote a mindset programme promoting positive thinking. Even at her age, she'd realised this was important. The primary choice of a person under pressure or experiencing difficulties is to decide whether they will succumb to negative beliefs and thoughts or replace feelings of sadness, loss and anxiety with happiness and hope.

So, whenever something good or bad happens to you, remember that you can choose what to think because what you choose to think will affect the outcome you get.

Event + Response = Outcome

Our thoughts create our reality

You may have heard this phrase before and not paid it much attention, but many studies have shown that the way we think does affect what happens in our life. Harvard psychologist Dr Ellen Langer's 'Reversing Ageing Experiment' shows this in action, revealing that positive thinking can affect someone's state of health when in old age.

The research took place in 1979 when Dr Langer recruited a group of men in their 70s and 80s. The men were told they were going to spend a week at a retreat in Boston reminiscing. When they arrived, they were split into two groups.

The first group, the control group, really did spend their time reminiscing about life in the 1950s. The second group was the research group and they had a different experience.

Instead of simply reminiscing, they were surrounded by props from 1959. They were asked to dress in clothing from that year, read magazines and watch TV shows from that time. They were also requested to discuss events from that year in the present tense. These events included Castro marching on Havana and the launch of the latest NASA satellite into space.

Dr Langer believed that if she could connect their minds with a period when they were at least 20 years younger, then they would think 'younger thoughts' and so become physically younger.

To support the idea that the men were younger, Dr Langer deliberately didn't install grab rails or gadgets aimed at helping older people complete everyday tasks, like showering. She also made sure the men were never treated as if they were sick or incompetent in any way.

HOW A NEGATIVE EMOTION IS CAUSED

A Distressing Memory or Thought

Causes

A disruption or "short circuit" in the body's energy system
(i.e. The meridian system)

Which, in turn,

Causes...

The negative emotion

Before the study began, Dr Langer met each one of them to check that they were suitable for the study. She noted that many of the men were frail. Yet, during the experiment the second group began to walk faster. In fact, they behaved more confidently in a number of ways; they even started to make their own meals. On the last day, one man even chose to put away his walking stick because he no longer felt he needed it.

In addition to the anecdotal changes she noticed, Dr Langer also gathered scientific data to test her hypothesis. She took physiological measurements before and after the experiment and these revealed amazing transformations in the men in the research group.

For example, her data revealed that the gait, dexterity, speed of movement, cognitive ability and memory of all the men in the experiment measurably improved. Their blood pressure went down, their eyesight and hearing improved and their arthritis became less severe.

As a result of the study, both groups of men showed physical and mental improvements, but it was the second group that improved most markedly. By encouraging the men to think as if they were younger, Dr Langer believes their bodies followed suit. So, they actually did become younger.

This is just one of many studies that have shown how the mind can have an impact on the body, aiding healing and improvements. In fact, some studies show that recovery can even occur when a placebo is used. You will have heard this referred to as the 'Placebo Effect'.

Our awareness of what is wrong with us, and our understanding of what is supposed to happen to us when we are given certain medicines or treatments, seems to be able to direct our brain and body to release the right chemicals and activate or deactivate our genes to stimulate the relevant recovery.

This doesn't only apply to physical health and healing, though. It also means we have the power to shape our perceptions, and that means we can see our experiences differently. So, we can change our lives simply by changing the way we think.

We can therefore change our life by choosing whether to develop our positive or negative thoughts. When you realise the truth of this for yourself, you'll find it easier to change the way you think. That change in your thinking will, in turn not only change the way you behave but also the way you feel.

So, the first step is to notice what you're thinking because if you don't do that, you can't take meaningful action. Next, let's look at the types of thinking that could make a difference in your life.

Turning negatives into positives

One of the first steps you need to take if you're going to turn your life around is to recognise and overcome your limiting beliefs because they will only hold you back and keep you stuck. Beliefs are deep-seated in our psyche and often difficult to identify because they usually take root in our psyche when we're very young. The very first belief you need to be aware of and remove is the one that tells you that you can't do what you want or that you're helpless.

In 2004, a study by scientists Hess, Hinson and Statham at North Carolina University revealed that priming participants with certain words led to them believing those words then acting accordingly.

The study was centred around stereotyping and memory. As with Dr Langer's work, the participants were elderly. Some of the group were primed with words such as 'confused', 'cranky', 'feeble' and 'senile', whilst others received 'accomplished', 'active', 'dignified' and 'distinguished'.

The results in simple terms were that those who received the more positive words did much better in the memory tests than those who had been primed with the negative words. This again supports the idea that positive thinking influences outcomes.

Of course, changing your thoughts and limiting beliefs isn't easy, and although you can't eliminate them overnight, it can be done. For instance, when I was told Liora would die on 19 April 2016, it would have been very easy for me to believe: 'There's nothing I can do, that's what they said, that's what will happen.' But instead, I chose not to be limited by this belief and to take action. As a result, she lived for another 12 days.

Although Liora has left us, I choose to believe: 'I can talk to Liora anytime, anywhere.' You may choose to believe something different, such as: 'I have to go to the cemetery to talk to the dead.' That's fine, but it's not a belief that serves me.

Next, explore your limiting beliefs. Where do they come from? How are they holding you back? Write your answers below:

Three limiting beliefs I have are:

i...

....

ii..

....

iii...

....

These stem from:

....

....

....

....

....

They hold me back by:

....

....

....

....

....

I often hear people say they can't do something. They say they've tried to do it before, but it hasn't worked. What matters, though, isn't what happened before, but what we do right now. To use a driving analogy, it's like driving forward while looking in your rear-view mirror. Eventually, you'll crash because you're not looking where you're going. They need to focus on what they can do today, not on what happened yesterday.

Think for a moment: if you had told your great-grandfather that you'd be able to do the following things, would he have believed you?

- Do your shopping without leaving the house.

- Pay for things without physically having money.

- Carry a phone with you all day.

- Listen to your favourite music while walking down the street.

- Cook and heat food in a matter of minutes without using the oven.

- See and speak to relatives thousands of miles away whilst sitting in your living room.

- Expect to live into your 90s.

What your great-grandfather would have thought impossible is now possible. So why limit yourself by telling yourself that what you want to do can't be done? When you think the right thoughts and instil the right beliefs, you really can do anything.

'We learn our belief systems as very little children, and then we move through life creating experiences to match our beliefs. Look back in your own life and notice how often you have gone through the same experience.'

Louise Hay

Negative and limiting beliefs usually start when we're very young – even babies – but some can take hold later in life too.

These beliefs often have a detrimental effect on our whole life – if we let them.

Children are often taught by their parents that the world is a scary place. They're told not to talk to strangers and not to stand out. This is how children learn to be fearful, expect the worst and limit themselves.

Their parents are, of course, just trying to protect them and teach them to be careful and responsible adults. Hopefully most of us, if we actually take the time to stop and think, realise that most people are generally good and will treat us as we treat them.

Society also indoctrinates us to believe we have a duty to collect material things and in order to do this, we must work really hard and become superior to others. But, by believing this, we limit ourselves and miss out on wonderful opportunities.

There is a part in the story of *Snow White* that reminds us of how what we believe becomes our reality. It's when Snow White is lying in the forest crying. She starts to believe there are lots of eyes staring at her. She's right, there are, and they belong to the forest creatures. But she doesn't see them. When she raises her head to look at the birds, squirrels and deer, all she sees is the deep, dark, unmoving forest because this is what she is focusing on: being lost in the forest. This shows how focusing on one idea can lead us to miss out on the infinite possibilities offered to us by the energy field.

Remember that your thoughts create your reality, and that means you alone create your reality. It's an empowering thought, because it means you can rewire your brain and free yourself from your conditioning. The minute you make an intention, you create it. Thoughts are vibrational waves and your thoughts draw in other matching vibrations.

It's just like turning on the radio, you can choose the channel that you want to listen to. But you can only hear the radio channel you want to hear when your thoughts are aligned to that channel. Walt Disney said: 'If you can dream it, you can do it,' meaning that if you can think it, you can make it happen.

Consider all the great inventions and sporting achievements that would never have happened if the individuals involved hadn't first believed they could do them. Maybe you know people who've harnessed the great power of positive belief that has led them to achieve great things. What could you learn from them?

Our thoughts and beliefs directly impact our actions. In fact, everything we do starts with a thought. This shows the power contained in our thoughts and beliefs. They're like seeds that determine what we do. So, if you change your beliefs about what you can do, you can change your results or outcomes.

This reminds me of the well-known saying: 'If you always do what you've always done, you always get what you've always got.' So, the truth is that if we want to change what we do so we can get a different outcome, we first need to change our thoughts.

With this in mind, let's look more closely at the concept of energy and vibration to see how we can use these elements to rid ourselves of limiting beliefs and move forward positively in our lives.

CHAPTER 6
OVERCOME YOUR NEGATIVE
THINKING

Our thoughts are vibrations, energy waves that interact and influence the field of possibilities. Every thought we have, have had and ever will have creates a vibration that extends out into the energy field. These vibrations criss-cross with other vibrations to create an incredible maze of energy that connects with matching vibrations. We are like living magnets that radiate thought-energy and we attract the people and events into our lives that align with our own significant thoughts.

For instance, have you ever thought about something you wanted or someone you needed to see, only to bump into them or get that thing shortly afterwards? You might see this as coincidence, but in fact, it is energy vibrations flowing as a result of our thoughts. You might know this concept as 'The Law of Attraction' or 'The Secret'.

Up to now, you may have believed that it was the situation you were in that resulted in your thoughts, but the reality is that it was your thoughts that created your situation.

Another illustration of how the Law of Attraction works is when you suddenly see a particular object everywhere. Let's say you're thinking of buying a car and specifically, a Volkswagen Golf. Because buying the car is on your mind, you see VW Golfs everywhere. This shows that what you think about expands – or to put it another way, you see what you think about because that's what you're focusing on.

Why does this happen? Well, it's because once we bring certain thoughts into our consciousness they can take over. While this can happen with positive thoughts, it most often happens with negative thoughts. So, when we focus on our negative thoughts, they take over and all we see is negativity. Our subconscious mind absorbs our thoughts and beliefs as if they are the truth, so it begins the process of causing our thoughts to become reality. That means that, if we focus on limiting beliefs, we get more evidence to convince us that they are true.

How to overcome negative thoughts and limiting beliefs

To move forward to something more positive, we need to take control of our minds and create beliefs and expectations that help us get what we want. Some examples of limiting beliefs include:

- I always make mistakes.

- I will never have enough money.

- I am not good enough.

So, how do we actually get rid of limiting beliefs? Here are some common techniques you can use.

Stop the negative thoughts

Before you can stop your negative thoughts and limiting beliefs, you need to notice them. That means you need to become far more self-aware. Negative thoughts are often easier to spot than limiting beliefs. That's because our beliefs are more ingrained in our thinking than our negative thoughts. When you notice your negative thoughts, repeat the words 'release' or 'cancel' or 'let it go' to stop the thought or belief in its tracks. Finally, replace that belief with a completely different positive thought before it takes root.

Name it

Next, name the limiting belief by simply telling yourself: 'That's a limiting belief.' You don't need to do anything else because negative thoughts and limiting beliefs only have power if you take action as a result of them. So, name it, don't get trapped by it, let it go and move on to something more positive.

Exaggerate it

This technique acknowledges that limiting beliefs are part of distorted thinking. When you notice the limiting beliefs creeping in you, catch them and turn them into something hugely exaggerated.

So, for example, when you think 'I'm no good at relationships,' this could become: 'Every relationship, whether romantic, family-based or with friends or work colleagues, has been a complete disaster.' When you exaggerate in this way, your logical mind will object and tell you this can't possibly be true.

Some therapists and coaches advocate taking this technique to an even greater extreme by suggesting you exaggerate your statement to make it completely ridiculous. For example: 'The next time I go out on a date, the man I meet will dress like a clown and throw a custard pie at me – and then I'll slip over and get smothered in it.' When you create this ridiculous vision, it'll make you laugh and stop thoughts taking hold.

Do the exercise below, so you can start to identify your own limiting beliefs and try out some techniques to see which ones work for you:

Write down one limiting belief that you hold:

....

....

....

Now think about how you are going to go about removing this limiting belief using the 'Stop' Technique:

....

....

....

Next, try the 'Name It' Technique. Did you find this useful or not? Why?

....

....

....

Now try the 'Exaggerating' Technique. Think of a ridiculous story that makes you laugh and write it down here:

....

....

....

What positive thought did you use when you exaggerated further and how did it help?

....

....

....

....

....

Focus on the positive

When you catch yourself focusing on your negative thoughts or limiting beliefs, you need to counteract it by thinking the opposite. So: 'I'm no good at relationships' becomes 'I'm great at relationships.' By thinking the positive thought, you take the power out of the negative one.

All of these techniques aim to take the power away from your limiting beliefs and prevent them from engulfing you. Unfortunately, most people do the complete opposite: the thought comes to mind, they focus on it, worry about it and as a result it manifests, which once again strengthens the limiting belief. The way to success is to practise and repeat these techniques and use them in conjunction with the other tools in this book.

The first step is to notice what you are thinking. With my clients, I often suggest that they wear an elastic band or bracelet on their wrist and then, when they notice that they are having a negative thought or limiting belief, I ask them to move the band or bracelet to the other wrist. This reinforces their awareness and is the first step towards taking action and being in control.

In the same way that identifying and changing limiting beliefs helps, changing the language of your thoughts can help too. This is often referred to as reframing and, in a way, is the opposite of exaggeration as it gives a new perspective on situations and stops them becoming limiting beliefs. So, you can reframe beliefs like 'I always make mistakes' – a thought that stops you trying anything for fear of getting it wrong – to 'sometimes I make mistakes,' which helps you stay balanced and remember that sometimes you are successful and could try something without being in fear of making mistakes.

You may want to reflect on this further. For example, the reason why you make mistakes with a task is that you don't have enough time, are lacking some knowledge or maybe have other stresses that lead you to lose concentration. Understanding this will give you insight, which could lead you to taking an appropriate action to stop this happening again. Other examples of reframing include:

- 'Nothing ever works for me' could become 'Life is full of ups and downs.'

- 'I'm no good at relationships' could become 'that last relationship with x didn't work out but I have a good relationship with y.'

Again, you may need to do some further research to identify the reasons why the relationship didn't work out and then you could take some actions that could lead to better outcomes in future relationships. You can also change individual words that have a negative connotation into more positive ones, such as:

- 'Failed' to 'Learned'

- 'Lost' into 'Searching'

- 'Problems' to 'Challenges'

- 'Should' to 'Could'

Remember, you create your own meaning, but the second versions are certainly more empowering than the first.

Reframing your thoughts in this way stops what might be called your 'all or nothing' thinking. This helps you move away from your current position because you gain the confidence to take positive action.

Perhaps you can think of some phrases or words that you commonly use which are negative and which hold you back.

 Write them below, and then reframe them into something more empowering.

NEGATIVE	POSITIVE

Affirmations

The use of affirmations was popularised by French psychologist Emile Coué in the 1920s. I've been using them myself. I have them displayed around my house and all my children, including Liora, have grown up with them. I move them around and add new ones from time to time. The girls notice and comment on them: 'Oh, I see you've put a new one on the cupboard.'

Research supports my belief that positive affirmations can make a difference to what we experience and achieve. For example, a 2013 study by five staff at Carnegie Mello University suggested that a brief self-affirmation activity at the start of the school term boosted the average end-of-term scores of previously underperforming children. This experiment looked at the use of affirmations to boost a stressed individual's problem-solving abilities.

An affirmation is a way of talking to your subconscious, replacing negative thoughts with positive ones. When we think negative thoughts, we create negative experiences. An affirmation inspires and motivates us and opens the door for many more positive thoughts.

If you fill your mind with positive thoughts, you'll gradually develop a positive mental attitude. When you do that, your mind starts to view your optimistic thoughts as reality because your subconscious mind can't differentiate between what you imagine and what's real.

When you use affirmations, you reprogramme your mind to create positive mental images that reinforce your overall attitude. Regular use also helps you stay focused on your goals. As a result, you're likely to feel more energised, which will make it easier to achieve your goals.

Of course, repeating affirmations is only part of the process. The secret to achieving maximum success from them is to prepare an atmosphere in which your positive thoughts can develop and grow. Affirmations are like seeds and if you plant them in poor soil, they won't grow. If you plant them in rich soil, they'll grow big and strong. The more you choose to think thoughts that make you feel good, the more likely you will feel good.

It's also important that you state clearly what you want rather than focusing on the problem, otherwise you'll simply reinforce the problem rather than creating the solution.

Regular use of affirmations will make you feel lighter and happier and so help you generate yet more good things in your life. It's a positive cycle: positivity leads to better experiences and outcomes and this in turn leads to yet more positive thoughts.

Best of all, you can create affirmations for any area of your life, from your relationships and health to your work and money, helping you attract more of what you want into your life. If you have negative thoughts about money, such as 'I'm useless at saving money,' you might create an affirmation to counter it, such as 'saving money comes easily to me.'

If you have negative thoughts about your weight, you might find yourself thinking: 'I'm so overweight, I just can't seem to shift the pounds.' In this case, your affirmation might be: 'I manage my weight easily and feel great.'

By using affirmations, you are demonstrating to yourself and your unconscious mind that you are taking responsibility and acknowledging that there's something you can do to make a change. You are making a decision to heal your life and move forward. When writing your affirmations, it's important you follow some key guidelines to make them as powerful and effective as possible.

- Express them in the present tense.

- Include positive words.

- Ensure they are specific to you.

- Repeat them to yourself regularly.

Repetition is important because it creates new neural pathways in the brain. When you state your affirmation in the present, your brain thinks it's true and already happening, helping make reality fit your thoughts.

Opinion is divided on the number of times you need to repeat your statement, but I suggest ten times in the morning and ten times at night is a good starting point. Alternatively, simply repeat an affirmation whenever a negative thought arises. See what works for you.

Affirmations are formed by expressing in positive terms what you want and saying it as if it has already happened. This can be difficult at first because your negative voice will pipe up and tell you it isn't true. If this is the case for you, include phrases such as, 'I am learning to…' or 'I am getting better at…'.

These phrases are still stated in the present tense, but they recognise progress and change. However, it's important that you avoid phrases like 'I am trying to' because often all you get is a lot of trying rather than achieving. Remember, our thoughts create our reality, so be careful what you think.

To reinforce your affirmations, say them out loud and read them as often as possible. Pin them to your fridge, mirror and computer and carry them around with you so you can read them throughout the day. Some of my favourite affirmations are:

- 'I'm grateful that everything in my life comes easily all of the time.'

- 'I'm so grateful that my body is creating perfect health.'

- 'I'm grateful for what I have. I happily count all my blessings.'

Affirmations are often seen as a self-help tool for adults, but Liora knew of their benefits and believed they would help teenagers cope with the changes and challenges of developing into an adult. So, when she was 18, she wrote '365 Daily Positive Affirmations for Teenagers.'

I knew they could help younger children too, so I created the 'Happy Child Affirmations Calendar'. Both are available via Amazon.

Now, keep practising so that using affirmations becomes an automatic part of your new daily routine. That way, they'll help you make positive, consistent changes in your life. You'll soon experience your mindset and beliefs being positively impacted. To help with this, get into a good routine with your affirmations by:

- Writing them down.

- Reading them to yourself.

- Saying them out loud.

- Listening to them via a recording.

- Believing them.

You can read some of Liora's affirmations around health and wellbeing below.

I love feeling active and positive.

I love creating a life of joy.

I allow a state of total wellness in my body. I choose to focus on thoughts of wellness.

I choose to believe that wellness is my right. Peace and comfort are within me constantly.

I choose to feel strong and healthy.

Now it's time for you to create some of your own affirmations.

1: What aspect of your life do you want to change?

....

....

....

....

2: How do you want it to change?

....

....

....

....

3: How will you feel when things change?

....

....

....

....

4: Now it's time for you to create your own affirmations, remembering to be positive and specific and write in the present tense.

....

....

....

....

....

....

....

....

....

Gratitude

I believe that expressing gratitude is a very important aspect of life. It's so easy to moan about what you don't have, but when you show your appreciation for what you have, you develop a far more positive mindset. It also helps you to stay focused on the present rather than waiting to be happy at some unspecified point in the future.

If you notice yourself using the phrase, 'I'll be happy when…,' you could end up waiting to feel happy until you experience a specific event, such as getting married, buying a house or having three holidays a year. When you spend too much time thinking about what you don't have, you'll start dwelling on the past and what you don't have now.

Alternatively, when you become future-focused, you begin to feel in control of your life, believing you can have more. Finally, expressing gratitude frees you from the regrets of the past because it helps you recognise that you're happy with what you have now.

Many independent research studies have revealed that practising gratitude has huge advantages for wellbeing. When researcher Amit Amin assessed over 40 research studies on gratitude, he discovered that there were more than 31 benefits covering five key life areas: personal, emotional, social, health and career. From this, he concluded: 'Gratitude is no cure-all, but it is a massively under-utilised tool for improving life satisfaction and happiness.'

So, my question to you is: If gratitude improves your happiness, why *wouldn't* you practise it?

I urge you to take time each day to acknowledge the good things in your life. Be grateful and say, 'Thank you.' Doing this will stop you worrying about the future. It'll give you an inner glow that will radiate from you. When you express gratitude, you'll gain a sense of peace and freedom.

Again, remember that what we focus on expands and becomes our reality, so if you constantly fret about what you don't have, you'll simply feel overwhelmed and disappointed. If you think about and celebrate what you do have, you'll experience a sense of abundance. You're also far more likely to attract good things into your life.

 Are you already starting to form a list of things and people you are grateful for? Write some of them down below.

I am grateful for:

....

....

....

....

As I said earlier, I could have chosen to feel angry and resentful about Liora passing away so young and so suddenly. Instead, I choose to be grateful for the 20 years I did have with her and to appreciate her inspiring legacy. Gratitude, rather than bitterness, is enabling me to move forward with my life rather than being paralysed by hurt and sadness.

If you are struggling to come up with things you are grateful for, it's a good idea to start with what you take for granted. That might be the people around you such as your friends, family and colleagues. It could be the things you have, including your home or car. Up to this point, you may have spent a lot of time criticising and finding fault with them, but if they were in danger, you'd do everything possible to help them. It's easy to take those closest to us for granted because they're always there. In fact, their presence is woven into the fabric of our daily life to such a degree that they become part and parcel of it and part of any difficulties we're experiencing. It's easy to mistake the ones we love for the problems in our life. When we take a step back, though, we can see that the people we love bring us joy rather than problems.

On the occasions since Liora's passing when I've felt down, one of the things I've done is to stop for a moment and write down five things I'm grateful for. This, along with the other tools, has quickly transformed my mindset and thought patterns from the negative to the positive. Now, I can express gratitude with ease. Off the top of my head, here are a few things I'm currently grateful for right now:

- I'm grateful that I had Liora for 20 years.

- I'm grateful that the hospital allowed me to use my holistic techniques, play music and bring Whisky (our dog) in to see Liora. (I don't think this would have been allowed in some countries).

- I'm grateful for having my other daughters.

- I'm grateful for my husband.

- I'm grateful for being healthy.

- I'm grateful for all I have.

By practising gratitude, you too will be able to recognise the gift of life at the deepest level. It'll open you up to the realisation that everything is sacred – every moment, every person, everything in the world. You'll see that every day is precious. If you normally grumble when your alarm clock goes off each day, instead be grateful that you are alive and have another day ahead of you with all the opportunities it has to offer.

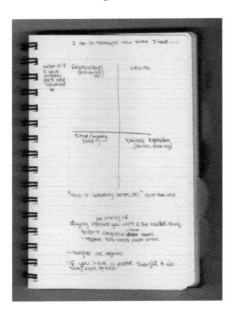

Here's an example from one of Liora's notebooks

I sometimes hear mothers at the school gates saying what a nuisance it is to have to pick up their children or complaining that they've got to go home and make dinner.

I had a friend who didn't work because she wanted to take her child to school and be there for him at the end of the day. Some mums said she was wasting her life being a stay-at-home mother. There was a lot of judgment of her choice. Then, suddenly, she died of cancer and she wasn't there anymore. I think somehow, deep down, she knew she didn't have a lifetime to do these things, so she made sure she did them while she could.

So many people take for granted what they have every day, thinking it's just normal. I say, 'Be grateful.' It's not until you break an arm that you realise how hard it is to get dressed without being able to use it. Don't leave it too late to be grateful for what you have now.

To use a rather old-fashioned phrase: 'Count your blessings' because, when you do, it puts your problems into perspective. It helps you recognise how and in what ways you are lucky to have what you have. It helps you see that others have far less than you.

 In the previous exercise, you started to think about what you are grateful for. Now add a few more things to your list.

I am also grateful for:

....

....

....

....

Many people choose to write down a list of what they are grateful for every day in a gratitude journal. Some do this just before they go to bed and others when they get up in the morning. But there are no rules and, as I've said before, I sometimes write down what I'm grateful for during the day if I've had a negative thought.

If you find it hard to express gratitude at first, you can keep your list short – maybe even as short as two or three items. But once you start to do the exercises more regularly, you'll begin to feel lighter and happier, so writing longer gratitude lists will feel far easier.

Soon, your gratitude list will start to produce positive and fulfilling results in your life and you'll enjoy writing them. Other ways you can focus on gratitude include:

- Carrying a small physical item like a pebble, crystal or shaped object that reminds you of a thing or person you're grateful for.

Love, Light and Liora

- Instead of just writing a gratitude list, drawing a heart and writing what you're grateful for in the centre of it.

- When you write your gratitude statement, adding an explanation of what you value about that person, event, experience or object.

- When you notice that you're starting to complain about something, consciously stopping and looking for the positives in that situation.

- Telling someone that you appreciate them. Pick some of the qualities they have that you admire or things they've done that you're truly grateful for.

- Every day, acknowledging and thanking those who make you coffee and serve you in shops and restaurants.

- Going for a walk and making a note of everything you see on the way that you appreciate.

- Appreciating yourself.

- Making gratitude part of your family life by asking everyone to share what they're grateful for. A good time to do this is when you sit down for dinner.

Like all the tools in this book, it's regular practice of them that will bring the greatest shifts for you. So, work out the best ways for you to express gratitude and incorporate those practices into your daily life.

Unconditional love

I talked in the previous section about gratitude and appreciating those who share our lives with us. Now I want to take this one step further and explain to you the benefits of unconditional love.

For me, unconditional love means loving someone without expecting anything in return. This is certainly how I feel about Liora and all my girls and husband.

I've got five girls; Liora is in a different world but she is still one of my girls as her energy is with us. Energy never dies and nobody can ever take away the memories and the feelings I have for Liora.

The power of love cannot be knocked down by death. Our love for Liora, and I'm sure yours for your loved ones who have passed away, will always live on. I know healing takes time, but Liora will always be with us in our hearts.

As well as not expecting anything in return, I see unconditional love as being an acceptance of others without judgment and without wanting to control others.

I sometimes hear parents tell their children things like, 'If you pass your exams, I'll get you a car. If you do this, I will do that.' To me this isn't unconditional love: it is trying to control your child's behaviour and telling them you'll only love them *if* they succeed. To me, unconditional love remains, even when someone fails.

Indeed, a 2013 study at the University of California showed that a lack of parental warmth led to children feeling more stressed. Parents who put their children under too much pressure to succeed, without balancing this with affection, put their children at risk of health conditions like high cholesterol, cardiovascular problems and high blood pressure. Judith E. Carroll, lead author of the study, said that by contrast, 'if the child has love from parental figures, they may be more protected from the impact of the abuse on adult biological risks for health problems than those who don't have that loving adult in their life.'

Someone once said to me they didn't believe they should love someone unconditionally if that person has treated them badly or hurts them, and that loving someone 'whatever' is wrong.

My response to this is that in order to be treated badly you have to give the other person permission to do this – you have to allow it to happen. If you don't allow it, then you may have to walk away to protect yourself. I'm not saying you must love everyone unconditionally. No, you can choose whom to love. I'm not advocating unhealthy relationships at all.

Those you love unconditionally; you love in good times and bad times. So even though circumstances may change, your love for that person does not. There's a big difference between saying: 'I love you whatever happens,' and 'I love you no matter what you do to me.'

One is healthy, the other isn't.

Think about whom you love and whether your love is unconditional.

1: Whom do you love?

....

....

....

....

....

....

2: Is your love for them unconditional?

....

....

....

....

....

3: Who loves you unconditionally?

....

....

....

....

....

....

CHAPTER 7
MODERN ENERGY TECHNIQUES
(TAPPING)

In the ambulance on the first evening that Liora was ill, I used Modern Energy Techniques to help her. I had learned from my training with Karl Dawson that this technique – often known as 'tapping' – could help someone in distress.

I used it to rebalance Liora's energy flow and minimise any physical damage. This is because emotional or physical distress disrupts someone's energy flow. This energy flow is often referred to as the body's meridian system.

The origins of tapping date back over 5,000 years to the Ancient Chinese Shoalin and Taoist monasteries when the body's meridian points were first mapped. Since then, the technique has been developed and refined by George Goodheart, Roger Callahan and Gary Craig.

Tapping is similar to acupuncture in that it focuses on the meridian lines. The difference is that tapping is used to stimulate the meridian lines instead of needles. It's a mind/body healing technique that combines the physical benefits of meridian treatments with the mental effects of simultaneously focusing on the pain or problem that is causing distress.

During tapping, users mentally 'tune in' to specific issues they're experiencing and send calming messages to the brain whilst at the same time tapping certain meridian points on the face, upper body and hand with their fingertips. This allows them to release emotional issues, so the body can repair itself quickly. The technique often results in a reduction in symptoms or the removal of the problem altogether. One of its many advantages is that it can deliver results in minutes or hours rather than months or years.

When you tap on your meridian points, you send kinetic energy through your energy system, clearing blockages and allowing energy to flow freely again. Tapping literally wakes up your energy system, which you experience as positive emotions or a reduction in physical distress.

Tapping can be used to help a wide range of issues, including addiction, anxiety, depression, fear, grief, guilt, insomnia, pain, physical illness and sexual abuse. Tapping is relatively easy to learn, so why not try it? Begin by focusing on a problem you have right now. The basic methodology is set out below.

Step 1

Before you begin, consider the intensity of your problem using a subjective 1-10 scale. Strong distress would be an 8, 9 or 10 while a minor issue might be a 2, 3 or 4. The name of this score is Subjective Units of Distress Scale or SUDS.

So, thinking about the problem you currently have, what is your current SUDS? Write down that number. Next, you need to form a Set-Up Phrase. This phrase should relate directly to the issue you want to work on. Say the Set-Up Phrase out loud three times while tapping on a meridian point (see page 103).

To get you started, there are some examples of Set-Up Phrases on the next page:

- 'Even though my back aches, I deeply and completely accept myself.'

- 'Even though I have a fear of heights, I deeply and completely accept myself.'

- 'Even though I get angry at work, I deeply and completely accept myself.'

Be as specific as possible when describing your issue or problem. Saying 'even though I have this stabbing pain on the top of my left shoulder...' is better than, 'even though I am in pain.'

 When your Set-Up Phrase is right, write it down so that you don't forget it.

Write down your Set-Up Phrase:

....

....

....

The meridian points

There are 14 meridian points used for tapping. On the following pages, there is a description of each one, along with a diagram showing where they are located on the body.

0 = The Sore Spot – The area on your chest where you'd pin a medal or a brooch. Use your fingertips to push gently until you find a place that feels tender rather than sore.

1 = Start of the Eyebrow – Where the bone behind your eyebrow turns into the bridge of your nose.

2 = Corner of the Eye – On the bone, in the corner of your eye.

3 = Under the Eye – On the bone just below your eye and in line with your pupil when you're looking straight ahead.

4 = Under the Nose – Between your nose and your upper lip.

5 = Under the Mouth – In the indentation between your chin and your lower lip.

6 = Collarbone – In the angle formed by your collar-bone and the breastbone.

7 = Under the Arm – In line with a man's nipples on the side of the body.

8 = Thumb – All finger points are on the side of the finger, in line with the nail bed.

9 = Index Finger

10 = Middle Finger

11 = Little Finger

12 = Karate Chop Point – On the opposite side of your hand to your thumb, roughly in line with your 'lifeline'.

13 = Gamut Point – Just behind and between the knuckles of your ring and little finger.

14 = Top of the Head – On the crown of your head.

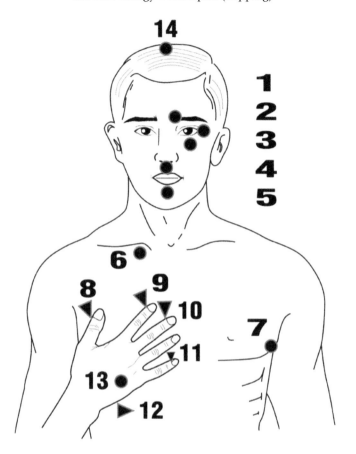

Step 2

Now, whilst holding onto the problem, tap around seven times on each of the meridian points. At each point repeat a shortened version of your Set-Up Phrase, which is known as the Reminder Phrase.

Examples include:
'This backache.'
'This fear of heights.'
'This irritability at work.'

This step is sometimes referred to as 'The Round' because it involves going around the sequence of meridian points many times.

Step 3

Now move onto tapping the Gamut Point. This can be found on the back of the hand in between the knuckles of your ring and little finger. Tap here and carry out the following actions to engage the two hemispheres of the brain and get your neurology working on your problem.

Repeat your Reminder Phrase once while you:

- Tap with your eyes open.

- Tap with your eyes closed.

- Tap while looking down and left.

- Tap while looking down and right.

- Move your eyes in a clockwise semi-circle.

- Move your eyes in an anti-clockwise semi-circle.

Next:

- Hum about five notes of a song (this engages the creative side of your brain). Any song will do but many people use 'Happy Birthday'.

- Hum five notes of a song again.

- Count 1-9 quickly to engage the left (logical) side of your brain.

Step 4

Repeat Steps 1, 2 and 3.

Step 5

You may have complete relief from your distress now (determine this by using SUDS). If your distress has reduced but not gone, repeat the sequence with some adjustments.

What is your SUDS now?

....

....

....

1. Make a slight change to the Set-Up Phrase

This acknowledges that there has been some improvement: 'Even though I still have some of the (insert problem), I deeply and completely accept myself.' So, if you had a fear of heights, this would be: 'Even though I still have some fear of heights, I deeply and completely accept myself.'

What is your adjusted Set-Up Phrase?

....

....

....

2. Alter the Reminder Phrase

This will reflect what's remaining about the issue, so the phrase becomes: 'This remaining (insert problem).' For example, fear of heights would become: 'This remaining fear of heights.'

> What is your adjusted Reminder Phrase?
>
> ....
>
> ....
>
> ....

At the end of this five-step sequence, your Subjective Units of Distress Rating (SUDS) should have reduced.

Your goal is to get your SUDS down to 0 or 1, which would indicate that you now have complete relief from your distress. This often happens for anyone who has up to an initial rating of 8. If your distress has not gone, do as many rounds as it takes to clear out the problem. Be persistent: it will take longer for some issues.

> What is your SUDS rating now?
>
> ....
>
> ....
>
> ....

Proxy Tapping

As well as tapping for yourself, you can also tap for someone else, as I did for Liora when she was suddenly ill. This means you tap on yourself to bring healing to another person.

This is known as proxy tapping. The Reminder Phrase in these instances is: 'Even though (insert name and problem/s), he/she deeply and completely accepts himself/herself.'

You can even use tapping on animals. We use it on our dogs when they are scared of fireworks or nervous about something.

Tapping is a tool that can help you in many ways, so do experiment. Even if you don't think tapping is applicable for your particular needs, try it anyway – you might be pleasantly surprised.

Here, I'm tapping on Liora

Silvia Hartmann's Positive Tapping technique

This technique builds on the idea of the need to create good energy flow. But, unlike the previous method, Positive Tapping focuses on bringing something we want into our lives (or bringing more of something we want into our lives), rather than working on eliminating a problem.

The underlying philosophy of Positive Tapping is that 'the better the energy flow in any body, the better the person becomes.'

For this technique, a scale called the Energy Body Stress Table is the form of measurement instead of SUDS.

Energy Body Stress Table

The Energy Body Stress Table has a scale that runs from -10 to +10.

The negative numbers

The negative numbers represent stress and disruption to the energy flow. So, -4 indicates general stress, which could be apparent when you experience lapses in the ability to control your thoughts, emotions and behaviour. At the end of the scale, -10 represents such extreme stress that the body shuts down.

The positive numbers

The positive numbers indicate levels of energy. That means +2 could be described as low energy, for example. This is possibly the way you feel when you've just woken up.

By contrast, +7 is very fast-flowing energy, which may be demonstrated by expanded awareness and feeling positive emotions such as love. So, a higher positive score indicates improved mental, physical and emotional states.

When your energy levels are low, it's as if you're trying to live your life on a low-charged battery. This makes everything feel as if it's hard work or difficult. If you keep pushing yourself when your battery is low, you're at risk of becoming ill.

So, raising your energy will not only make you feel better, it'll also help you develop a more positive outlook on yourself, others and the world. Positive energy lifts us to emotional states, helping us be at our best both physically and emotionally.

For Positive Tapping, the first question you need to ask yourself is: 'What energy form (feeling) do I need to bring into my life right now to make me feel better (or even better)?'

Once you've decided on this, the process is similar to traditional tapping, except that there are some extra points you need to tap on. These are on the top of your thumb, index finger, middle finger, ring finger and little finger.

Write down what type of energy you want to bring in:

....

....

....

So, why not follow along, inserting that energy feeling you want more of. There are many to choose from. I frequently choose joy, peace, love, hope, faith, health, focus, strength, success and trust. When I was at the hospital, I used Positive Tapping to bring me calm.

The Positive Tapping technique

1. Start with your hands crossed over on your chest and take three deep breaths.

2. Next, say out loud what you want more of in your life: for example, 'I want more love.'

3. Tap with your index finger on every meridian point, repeating your requested energy type strongly on each point. For example, 'love'.

4. Cross your hands back on your chest and consider whether you feel any different.

When you tap, do it lightly and rhythmically. Make sure you breathe in and out after each round of tapping. Stay relaxed throughout. Really think about the positive emotion you are tapping for and allow yourself to feel the emotion.

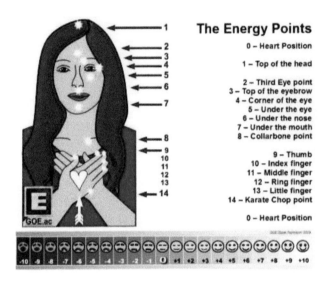

The Energy Points

0 – Heart Position

1 – Top of the head

2 – Third Eye point
3 – Top of the eyebrow
4 – Corner of the eye
5 – Under the eye
6 – Under the nose
7 – Under the mouth
8 – Collarbone point

9 – Thumb
10 – Index finger
11 – Middle finger
12 – Ring finger
13 – Little finger
14 – Karate Chop point

0 – Heart Position

- Check the SUE Scale and pick a number.
- 0 - The Heart Position. Point to yourself in the centre of your chest. Place your leading hand over this point, then place your other hand on top. Take three deep breaths, in and out. Say out aloud what you will be tapping on. For example: I want more energy.
- 1 – 14 - Now tap all the points lightly, starting at the top of the head and ending with the Karate Chop point. Use the index finger of your leading hand. Pause between each point and take one deep breath in and out.
- 0: Return to the Heart Position and take three deep breaths in and out.
- Check the SUE Scale.
- Tap more rounds of Energy EFT until you get to +10.

Energy EFT On A Page – Created by Silvia Hartmann for The Guild of Energists GOE.ac
Translated by your local energist.

Again, this is a mind/body technique. We engage the mind by speaking the words and we engage the body through touch as we tap. At the same time, we stimulate our energy system.

You can go further with this technique if you wish by doing more rounds of tapping and concentrating each time on your positive desire. However, make sure you change the phrase each time to raise your energy. So, if your original word was 'love', in subsequent rounds you could say 'more love' or 'even more love'.

With both traditional tapping and Positive Tapping, I've found that I can get a stronger impact if I look in the mirror as I do it. Look in the mirror, into your own eyes and say out loud what you want for yourself.

It's very powerful. Remember, at all times, to acknowledge the negative statements or messages that come up too, but do not give them too much importance and ensure that you really emphasise the positive.

To get the most benefit from this technique, ensure that you are well hydrated when practising any form of tapping. This is important because water conducts electricity and accesses the electrical energy that flows through our minds and bodies.

Take the time to really tune in to what you are about to do. Most people do this by crossing their hands on their chest and taking three deep breaths.

If you wear glasses or a watch, make sure you take them off as these could create interference with the flow of energy.

Seek help from a practitioner if you are struggling to get the results you want on your own or feel free to get in touch with me via my website or by email. I run tapping classes online.

CHAPTER 8
COLOUR THERAPY

Colour is a form of energy that we can actually see. It is basically light made up of photons that has different wavelengths and frequencies. Each colour has its own specific wavelength and frequency, and because of this, it also has its own specific properties that can be used to affect the energy and frequencies within our bodies.

Colour is all around. You'll probably already be familiar with using it in different ways. For instance, you can tell when certain fruits are ripe based on what colour they are – when a banana is yellow for instance, compared to when it is green.

There are holistic ways you can use colour to enhance your life too. Colour therapy (also known as chromotherapy) is a form of holistic healing that uses the visible spectrum of light and colour to affect a person's mood and physical or mental health.

In 1958, US scientist Robert Gerard conducted a study in which he claimed that red stimulates us and makes us anxious while blue promotes calm. He also showed how colour could affect appetite, blood pressure and levels of aggression. The colour blue is generally associated with calm and helps to lower blood pressure, while red has the effect of raising blood pressure.

Used in the right way, colour energy can be extremely powerful for healing. Although colour is largely perceived via the eyes, it is also believed that it can be perceived through our skin, helping to activate certain hormones that promote healing.

Practices that use colour in therapy are known to have existed for thousands of years. The Ancient Egyptians, for example, used colour as a cure for particular ailments and based their choice of colour on different parts of their buildings, depending on their properties and associations. For example, yellow represented the sun which they worshipped; green represented nature, and they used blue to represent the sky.

A Chinese medical book called the *Nei Ching*, which is over 2,000 years old, also records a form of diagnosis system based on colour. The medical profession continues to look at the use of colour via Photodynamic Therapy when dealing with particular cancers.

Today, common ways of using colour include the use of white and blue light to help people who suffer with Seasonal Affective Disorder, and the use of specific colours for decorating certain rooms in a house. It's also used in advertising to elicit desired responses and emotions from specific audiences.

We choose to wear particular colours because of their associations with certain ideas and feelings. For example, we wear black to denote authority and white to express purity.

Even hospitals and prisons are now beginning to think more carefully about the colours they use on walls and ceilings. That's because they've begun to realise that certain colours can affect how people feel. They can enable prisoners to feel calmer and patients to heal.

Have you used any specific colours in your home to achieve a certain mood? If so, list them on the next page.

Colour	Effect

Do you find certain colours irritating or associate them with negative experiences? Share these below:

Colour	Effect

I regularly use a range of colour therapies on myself and my clients. Liora worked with colours too.

Calling in a colour

You may recall that I wrote in Chapter 1 about how I used a form of colour therapy to improve the outcome of our meetings with Liora's medical team. In this form, you 'call a colour in' and visualise it to help solve a problem. I imagined a cloud of pink showering the medical staff and their legal advisers to make them more compassionate. I also worked on myself while I was at the hospital, I called in yellow for power and control to help me cope with what was happening, so I could stay focused.

I called in colours to help Liora when she was in the hospital too. For example, as blue represents healing, I imagined blue going into her body to soothe her and help her recover.

There are two key techniques for using colour therapy. The first is to visualise a cloud showering your own or another's body with colour. The other is to tune into another person's state and take it into your own body, like a surrogate. Then you pour the colour into yourself as a way of helping them.

Liora didn't like to take medicines or pain killers. Instead, she used colour therapy on herself. She used colours to relieve things such as period pain and headaches. Sometimes I would say, 'Go on, just take an Ibuprofen,' but she was very strong and would say no. She would send healing colours to the part of her body that was affected or where she felt there was an energy blockage, and the colours would help to release it and make the pain go away.

Colour in diagnosis

In addition to this way of calling in or asking for a colour, colour can also be used to delve into the root of an issue. So, a trained therapist might ask a client, 'What colour do you see or are you drawn to?' Or 'What colour represents the way you feel?' The therapist then uses the client's colour preference to help identify a particular problem before working with their client's energy to dispel negative feelings, to free blockages and restore balance in the body. It's also possible to combine asking someone about their colour preference with calling in a colour to help them. Colour therapist Pippa Merivale explains it like this:

'Colour is light; it throws light on things and shows you what you've not spotted in yourself, talents and gifts and hidden strengths, as well as the erroneous zones that it can help you to dissolve and flush out if you choose.'

I recently had a client who was a nine-year-old child. He used to get very angry and violent. I asked him what colour he thought the anger was. At first, he said he didn't know, but when I asked him to guess, he said it was red. I asked him where the colour was and he said it was in his heart, so we worked together to remove the red and replace it with a soothing colour.

Like other forms of energy therapy, working with colour in this way is totally holistic and non-invasive. That means it can be used with adults, children, babies and animals to help with emotional, physical, mental or spiritual issues. It can help with a wide range of problems too, from stress to immune deficiency problems and from insomnia to critical illness. You can also use it to aid relaxation.

Colour Mirrors

An advanced form of bringing in colour energy is the Colour Mirrors System. This was developed by Melissie Jolly in South Africa in 2001. This is an energy system used for healing, where colours are chosen to try to resolve a problem. The colours are represented by bottles of coloured and fragranced oils, each with its own distinctive essence. Some bottles even contain two colours.

When we were at the Royal London Hospital with Liora, I asked one of my daughters to bring me my Colour Mirror bottles from my office. I sprayed the scented oils around Liora's body, changing them each day depending on what I thought Liora needed. I used pink for love, purple for the soul and blue for healing. I also sprayed them on my husband and my other children to help them cope. I was very grateful they allowed us to use them in intensive care.

Each bottle has its own colour and scent, which really helps draw that colour into your body. When I use the Colour Mirrors System with clients and spray them with the oils, I ask them to take a deep breath in as the oil is transformed into a mist around them. This helps them experience the perfume and sensation of the oil so they can feel the colour entering their body. I hardly have to say anything at all to bring in the colour. If I can't use the sprays – maybe because I am working with a client online – I have to describe the colour in much more detail, but it still works, and I get the same results as spraying the oil on my client.

These bottles of oil can also be used to aid diagnosis as well as healing. Indeed, in the twentieth century, a long time before Jolly developed her Colour Mirrors System, colour therapy became popular as a result of the work of psychologist Dr Max Lüscher's Lüscher-Colour-Diagnostic Test. During the test, the recipient is asked to select eight coloured bottles in order of preference. The results are said to reveal a person's worries and offer a solution to their problems.

Other uses of the bottles include associating certain colours and bottles with astrology and birth dates to give readings.

Wearing colours

Another way I use colour to influence my emotions is by wearing it. Choosing your clothes based on their colour is an extremely proactive way of using it to influence how you feel.

An example of this is that I chose to wear a royal blue scarf at Liora's funeral. People often wear dark colours at funerals, but I felt the need for something else. I also knew I had to cover my hair as a mark of respect during certain parts of the ceremony, but I didn't want to wear a hat. I only wear a hat when I go to a smart event.

I wanted to do things differently and I wanted to take something supportive with me, both for myself and for my husband, because unfortunately, my extended family were unable to be there. I had to be strong for my daughters too. The only thing I could rely on was my knowledge of how to heal and support myself.

So, I deliberately looked for a large scarf to help me. During the ceremony, I wrapped myself in the scarf, covering my head. I draped it around me, snuggling into it, a bit like cuddle therapy. It helped me stay calm during that very difficult experience. Blue is associated with calming and healing. In the cemetery, that scarf was my friend and helped me stay in control. I love it and keep it in a special place.

Have you chosen to wear specific colours on a certain occasion, maybe a funeral, a wedding, a job interview or a time when you had a difficult meeting?

How did wearing these colours make you feel? Use the box below to record your feelings.

Colour	Occasion	Feeling

You may have chosen to wear a certain colour because you feel more energetic in it. That might especially be the case with brighter colours. Psychologist Ingrid Collins is convinced that chromotherapy can affect our energy: 'We know that the cells of the human body are constructed from atoms and that each atom consists of particles of energy in constant motion. We are therefore, at the most fundamental level, made of energy and information, so when we add a particular colour we are adding energy into our lives.'

In her wish to give flowers to those in need, Liora was also acknowledging the powerful, positive and uplifting effect of their many colours on the recipients.

Colours all around

One very simple way to use colour to change your mood is to place different coloured pieces of paper around your home.

Often, when people feel sad, they don't notice colour because everything looks grey to them. But if you put four different pieces of brightly coloured paper in four different rooms, they would be forced to notice the colours. By bringing colour into their life, their mood can be lifted.

You can buy coloured paper in most craft shops and it's not expensive. It's a particularly good idea to put a piece of coloured paper in the bathroom because this is one place where you can guarantee that you'll see it every day.

It's also a good idea to wear bright colours when you visit someone who might be feeling sad or depressed as this will help lift their mood.

 Spend some time thinking about how you could use colour to lift or change your mood. Write down your ideas in the space below.

How could you use colour to change your mood?

....

....

....

....

....

....

....

....

....

....

....

There are many simple ways to use colour, including through the clothes you wear every day. When you're getting dressed, notice which colours appeal to you and use this to guide what you wear each day. It's a simple but effective way to incorporate colour therapy into your daily life.

Next, I'm going to help you start using the techniques and tools I've described so far. We'll also look at what may stop you from taking action to create a more positive life for yourself.

 Use the space below to begin to write down some of the ways you plan to use colour to help yourself and others.

Who do you know who could benefit from having some colour in their life?

....

....

....

....

....

....

How could you use colour to help yourself?

....

....

....

....

....

....

....

....

CHAPTER 9
GET STARTED

So far, you've heard how I use energy-based tools and exercises to help me feel positive and deal with my emotions. Now it's your turn to take action and start to enhance your life.

There are three main steps to making changes:

1. Notice when you feel certain emotions such as sadness, joy, loneliness or gratitude and become more aware of the objects, events, situations and people that are positive or negative for you.

2. Acknowledge how you're feeling rather than burying your head in the sand and pretending it is not happening.

3. Take action to transform yourself. Notice whether you feel ready for that or whether you are resisting. Are there things that are stopping you or holding you back from making consistent changes so you can lead a fulfilling and successful life?

Next, let's look at what might be happening to indicate that you're resisting change.

Excuses

My own life experience and the knowledge I have gained through working with clients have taught me that knowing the science is not enough. I have learnt that each person has their own unique health and life story. To be able to help them, I must understand them by looking at their journey and all the factors that influence their ability to make better choices.

The first step is to help each person to become aware of whether they are making excuses to avoid change. And if they are, to be aware of what those excuses are and why they use them. You may create excuses for not taking action too, but like everyone else, you have a choice as to whether you let them hold you back or not.

Time

Many of us want a quick fix when it comes to dealing with our problems (perhaps you do too?) but we are all individuals, so there is no one way that is right for everyone. The truth is that change takes time and time is one resource you feel you have too little of.

But, if you're honest, you know you waste time. Think about it: how much time do you spend a day browsing on your phone or laptop? How much time do you spend doing pointless tasks, procrastinating or making what could take five minutes last an hour? There's no judgement in this; we all waste time one way or another. But if you can figure out what wastes your time and how you're going to change that, you can start to spend more time on what's important to you.

When you know what takes up too much of your time – it could be anything from people, daily tasks and avoidance tactics to lack of planning – you can start to make changes.

What wastes your time? Use the box below to write down your time-stealers.

What are your time-stealers?

....

....

....

....

....

....

....

....

....

Now that you've done that exercise, think about how much time each day (or on most days) you could spend doing something more productive or something that moves you towards the life you want. It might be one hour, two hours, etc.

If you can free up a chunk of time like an hour or more, you might want to set it aside to meditate, exercise, read, paint, study or practise tapping or colour work.

Alternatively, if you can only free up a few minutes here and there, you might need to plan to do a number of small things to move yourself forward, such as expressing gratitude or saying some affirmations.

No matter how much or little time you have for yourself, try to use it each day to help you make positive changes in your life.

Fear

One reason why you might be holding back is fear. Many people don't like change because they live their life in fear.

We all have a choice when we wake up in the morning; we can choose to live our life in fear or in peace and faith. A thought-provoking description of FEAR is:

- False

- Evidence

- Appearing

- Real

But you don't need to be restricted by fear. You can learn to see it differently. The fastest way to turn the tables on fear is to change the way you think and behave. So, instead of harbouring doubt, have faith. Instead of giving in to 'do it tomorrow' mentality, you can make an effort to do it now. Believe you are resourceful and capable of achievement, that way you'll beat fear. This way, FEAR changes to become:

- Faith

- Effort

- Achievement

- Resourcefulness

If fear is holding you back, figure out why it has power over you. Maybe you get attention from others when you're afraid? Perhaps it helps you avoid taking risks? It could be helping you avoid potential rejection. Whatever the fear is doing, what's certain is that it's helping you stay in your comfort zone.

Use the space below to write down how giving into your fear is working for you.

> How is giving into your fear serving you?
>
> ....
>
> ....
>
> ....
>
> ....

You could make a promise to yourself that you'll no longer let excuses get in your way. Without excuses, you're free to be who you want to be.

Remember the work you did in Chapter 4 and that if you stay in your comfort zone and don't change, nothing will alter.

I don't want you to be there; I want you to move forward. Make a pledge now to let go of your excuses by saying out loud:

'I will no longer let excuses hold me back.
I let go of all excuses that I have created.
I choose to move forward and take action to build a better life.'

Examples could include running your own business, owning your own house, being part of a loving relationship or simply being the best at what you do.

You may want to make a note of this goal on your phone or on a sticky note that you can put somewhere prominent, so you see it easily and often. Whatever you do, make sure you look at it regularly. It'll keep you motivated and inspired to keep taking action.

Don't be shy about your goals or make them smaller because they seem difficult or even impossible right now. One of my goals is to be interviewed by Oprah Winfrey. That's a big goal for me but I'm happy to share it and own it so I can work towards achieving it.

In the next section, I have laid out my suggested fast-action steps that are designed to help you make positive changes quickly. But before you go through these and start planning how to incorporate them into your day, you need to set a goal for something you want to achieve in the near future.

 Before you start the Daily Action Plan, think about what you want to achieve. Set a goal to reach over the next few weeks.

Which goal would you like to focus on first?

....

....

....

....

Before you begin...

Although I've suggested an order in which you might want to do some of the recommended daily actions, you can adapt them to suit your own preferences and schedule. Remember, if you want to make change part of your daily life, you need to take consistent and persistent action.

I try to do certain activities at around the same time each day as this makes it much easier to stay on track. For example, I meditate every morning as soon as my alarm goes off. I know how beneficial this practice is for my well-being, so I've included it in my morning routine. This ensures that I do it. If I leave it until later in the day, other things could easily get in the way.

Quick Daily Action Plan

In the morning

1: Positive affirmation

First thing in the morning I say this positive affirmation:

> *Today is an amazing day*
> *Something awesome is going to happen today*
> *I am healthy*
> *I am happy*
> *I am confident*
> *I am positive*
> *I am blessed*
> *I am grateful*
> *I am courageous*
> *I am excited about today*

Remember, even if your affirmations don't feel true right now, just keep saying them as this will alter your energy.

 Look back at the affirmations you created earlier. Regularly add new positive statements so you keep your affirmations motivating.

Which positive affirmations are you going to say each morning?

....

....

....

....

....

2: Mirror exercise

If you have a problem with low self-esteem, lack of confidence or a poor self-image, you may want to do this mirror exercise.

Do you remember when I talked about the power of using a mirror to look into your own eyes earlier in the book? Well, when we look in the mirror, most of us criticise ourselves. We tell ourselves things like: 'My hair is a mess,' 'My nose is too big' or 'I'm a bad person because I get angry easily.' You may have been making the same critical comments to yourself your whole life. But where has it got you? It certainly hasn't added to your happiness.

So, make a promise to yourself that you'll change. Take time to tell yourself that you're a worthwhile, loveable person: someone who is willing to make changes and to acknowledge and love themselves.

You could say: 'I love the person I am becoming,' or 'I am strong and willing,' or simply, 'I love myself.' Whatever you do, remember not to dwell on past mistakes. You can't change what has already happened, but you can have an impact on your future.

Remind yourself of what you love about yourself when you look in the mirror. Say it out loud for an even greater impact.

What do you love about yourself?

....

....

....

....

....

At first, most people I work with find this exercise difficult, but with consistent repetition, it gets easier.

3: Think about colour

When you get dressed each day, think about what you have learned about the psychology of colour. What can you wear that will help make this a great day for you?

> Write down which colours and clothes will help you to feel more confident and successful:
>
> ....
>
> ....
>
> ....
>
> ....
>
> ....
>
> ....

Throughout the day

1: Use visualisation

Visualisation is a great way to motivate yourself to reach your dream, and it's easy to do. Just close your eyes and imagine yourself reaching your dream. Run a movie of yourself in your mind's eye and see yourself achieving your goal. If you find this difficult or don't 'see' anything initially, persevere, it gets easier with practice.

How does achieving your dream make you feel?
Describe what can you see, smell and touch.

....

....

....

....

....

....

....

....

....

....

....

....

....

....

....

Reconnect with your vision four times a day, each time tuning into the feelings you get when you see yourself achieving your goal.

At which four times of the day will you repeat your visualisation?

1 ....

2 ....

3 ....

4 ....

2: Create a Vision Board

In addition to these daily visualisations, you may wish to create a Vision Board to show the goals you want to achieve. As well as using it for specific goals, you may also want to use it to envision your perfect day.

3: Get motivated!

It's important to find time to do some motivational activities each day. You can use these either as a process to top up your energy and help you conquer the world or as a pick-me-up if you are having a particularly difficult or stressful day.

Look back to the information about the Energy Body Stress Table (see page 110) and think about how you're likely to perform when you have high or low energy. If you experience low energy at certain points of the day, it could be beneficial to plan one of these activities for those times. These activities will help you change your emotional state.

You may choose to do physical exercise or read a book of motivational speeches; it doesn't matter, as long as it motivates you and raises your energy. Some of the things I like to do include watching motivational films, listening to uplifting music and very simply having a laugh.

Motivational films

Here are 10 motivational films:

1. Whiplash

2. The Blind Side

3. The Pursuit of Happiness

4. Jobs

5. The Social Network

6. Moneyball

7. Forrest Gump

8. Rocky

9. Dangerous Minds

10. Invictus

Next, write down the films that motivate you.

Which films motivate you?

1 ....

2 ....

3 ....

4 ....

5 ....

6 ....

7 ....

8 ....

9 ....

10 ....

Uplifting music

Compile your own list of 10 songs that make you feel brighter and encourage you to stride forward. You can find lots of uplifting playlists on sites such as YouTube and Spotify.

What songs or pieces of music lift you up?

1 ....

2 ....

3 ....

4 ....

5 ....

6 ....

7 ....

8 ....

9 ....

10 ....

Laughter

There is a plethora of scientific evidence that reveals how good laughter is for our mind and body. So, do everything you can to have a laugh every day.

You could watch a comedy show, look at funny YouTube clips, meet with friends who make you laugh, go to a laughter yoga class or read a joke book. It doesn't matter, as long as it makes you laugh. Using the space on the next page, write down the people, memories or events that make you laugh.

Generally, adults laugh much less than children, who laugh many times a day. But why miss out on the benefits it can bring?

Write down 10 things, people or memories that make you laugh.

1 ....

2 ....

3 ....

4 ....

5 ....

6 ....

7 ....

8 ....

9 ....

10 ....

Mindful colouring

You may think of colouring as a child's game and not something that has any importance or relevance to you. But there has been a huge boost in the popularity of colouring in recent years, largely because of the benefits it brings.

One of the key benefits of this easy activity is that it reduces stress and anxiety, improves concentration and builds better motor skills. It also gives you something else to focus on other than your negative thoughts.

Even if you haven't done any colouring since you were a child, get some coloured pencils and have a go. It's fun and a great way to take your mind off your worries. I aim to do some colouring every day.

You can find colouring books for adults in many shops, get downloads online and there are also specialist phone apps. I prefer good old-fashioned paper and pencils.

'I Am Awesome' Colouring-in

If you don't have anything to colour right now, start by colouring the image below. As you can see, it has a positive message for you too.

At the end of the day

There are two things you can do to support change at the end of each day.

The first is to write down at least five things you're thankful for. You might want to buy a journal or special notebook for these.

Five things I am grateful for:

1 ....

2 ....

3 ....

4 ....

5 ....

The other thing you can do at the end of each day is to review your 'To-Do List' and create a new one for the next day.

Below is a wonderful daily 'To-Do List' that you can use as a starting point. I don't know who created it, but I love it.

My To-Do List for Today
Count my blessings.
Speak gently.
Love much.
Laugh a lot.
Let Go of what I can't control.
Work hard.
Be Productive.
Just Breathe and
be Kind.

Weekly Actions

As well as having a daily action plan, it's worth thinking about what you want to make time to do each week. Focus on what you enjoy doing and what you are passionate about.

I love to:

....

....

....

....

....

....

....

....

How could I spend more time doing what I love?

....

....

....

....

....

....

....

....

....

Spending time doing what you enjoy is good for your mind and body. It helps you perform better in every area of your life because your energy is higher and that leads to positive thoughts and emotions.

When things go wrong

You may find keeping to this routine difficult at times and inevitably people and events may try to knock you off course.

Often, when you change, those around you find it difficult to handle, usually because they're afraid of how it may affect their relationship with you. That can lead them to unconsciously sabotage and undermine your resolve and efforts. But if you become aware of this, continue with your plan of action and show you're determined to make changes. Build your own personal 'repair kit', so you're ready to cope when life gets difficult.

Make a note of what you plan to do if something happens during the day that makes you sad or unhappy. Look through the exercises on Positive Mindset, Tapping and Colour Therapy in this book to help you.

The techniques I will use to help me change my emotions are:

....

....

....

....

....

....

....

....

....

If you need some motivation to live more fully, consider these brilliant words by Oscar Wilde. I first heard them during a speech at a 90th birthday party.

'To live is the rarest thing in the world. Most people exist, that is all.

Choose a life that is imbued in meaning, that creates beauty and goodness, that understands there are some things that require sustained process and not immediate satisfaction and above all, that is filled with good deeds.

When one sits with you one feels as if there is no one else in the world you care about more, you make everyone you meet feel like they are the centre of your world. Even if things are looking bad, your optimism and faith gives us a sense of clarity. You are always present; you are always amongst us, even though we may be far away physically.

Your stature, though small, towers above us all, shining its light on us in every place, and at every time.

You have empathy, and you lead life quietly with humility and dignity.'

I would love someone to say this about me. What would you like someone to say about you?

How to get further help
I would love to hear how you get on with these techniques.

If you want to get in touch with me to share your experiences, you can post on my special Facebook group or find out how I can help you on my website.

Facebook Group
www.facebook.com/groups/loveLightandLiora/

Website
www.fear-busters.com

Join online tapping classes
lauren@fear-busters.com

PART 3:
LIORA

CHAPTER 10
CELEBRATING LIORA'S LIFE

The Facebook Group

When Liora became suddenly ill, a Facebook group called 'Do a Mitzvah in the name of Liora Rosenberg' was set up by Lauren Weinberg so we could update people about what was happening. The group quickly had over 15,000 members.

We received many messages of support from the group. The members, who came from all over the world, told us about some of the amazing things they were doing in Liora's honour. Many changed their profile picture to a pink heart with #pray4liora in the middle as a sign of their support.

This is a post written by Lauren Weinberg in January 2017:

'When I started this group in April 2016, when Liora was sick, on the direction of the Rosenberg family, I never thought in such a short space of time, that at its peak 15k members would join. It's a shame that tragedy brought us together, but it's amazing, the unity and kindness of everyone in this group. I wanted to share something with you. I think about Liora a lot, especially from the day of her stone-setting when the weather was miserable, when the rabbi conducted the stone-setting (the revealing of Liora's headstone) the sky opened, and a beautiful light shone through onto the pink stones around Liora's grave, and onto the beautiful wording that the family had so carefully chosen. I could really feel Liora was with us. Then the weather returned to the normal miserable rain that it had set out for that day. So many people have shown their generosity over the year and continue to do so.

Liora aged 18 months

Liora's birthday is coming up in January, so I ask you, as an amazing group all over the world, to join me and the Rosenberg family in doing a mitzvah or good deed for someone in the merit of Liora, to lead up to her birthday and to elevate her soul. Like the rain, Liora's passing was a miserable time: let the light of this group shine out, like it did with love when it shone down on Liora's headstone. Please post pictures or comment on what you have done. Even if you make an effort to smile at someone, just one person, your kind gesture can make a person's day. This was one trait amongst many that Liora possessed – chesed (kindness) – and she was always wanting to help people. Whether you knew Liora or got to know her through the power of this group, the one underlying unity of us to Liora is chesed (kindness).'

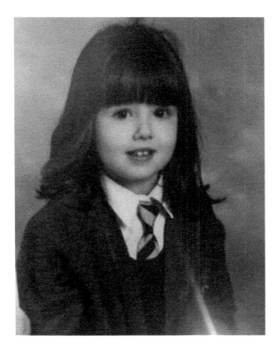

Liora starting reception class

Here are some of the Facebook messages that people sent around the time of Liora's passing. I've copied them exactly as they were sent:

LW: 16 May 2016

'It's amazing the love and unity, and amazing things that have come out of this group. Also, that if anyone needs prayers or help then we have shown as a group we will help. Please continue to do mitzvahs/good deeds in the name of Liora. Liora, as you can see, wanted to do so much in such a short lifetime, and had many ideas and started special projects that her amazing family can carry on – a Shabbos flowers gemach, prayers for others in need (look at the two boys from Stamford Hill, TG who are now awake), helping to donate an ambulance to Hatzolah, a calendar of positive affirmations to help teenagers, amongst other things that many didn't know about but soon you will – watch this space! You are all amazing! To the Rosenberg family, just to say, we will always be here for you. X'

CK: 10 May 2016

'This birthday is now special, and in the future when I will celebrate my birthday, it will make me feel so much closer to Liora Rosenberg. I will always miss you and think about you.

We had so many happy memories that I will treasure in my heart forever. Lauren Rosenberg, Judy Rosenberg, Fiona Rosenberg and the rest of the family, the memories we all had, I will treasure, and I know Liora is shining down on us, and will continue to. You are such a wonderful family, and I am always here for you. I love you all very much. Please fulfil Liora's wishes by helping us raise money for her chosen charity.

Liora also wrote a calendar with positive affirmation for teenagers which has been published, and you can buy it on Amazon. It is extremely inspirational, and she will always carry on inspiring me.'

AM: 8 May 2016

'Lauren, Stuart, and your beautiful girls! We came to shiva, and people are queuing outside and flooding the streets for you, including us, but because we cannot get to you, we want you to know we are thinking of you all, praying and sending all our love and light, and wish you all a long life. ♥'

SS: 6 May 2016

'My daughter and I lit an extra set of Shabbat candles for Liora. She did a unique thing for us all. Prayers for her soul to be rested, and her light to shine on her family for all their days xx, #light4liora'

LL: 5 May 2016

'Made these challahs [special Shabbat loaves] and said the bracha in Liora's name – that her precious soul be elevated to the highest possible place of rest where she may be able to continue to shine brightly.

We lived on the same street, and I'll always remember her sweet smile as we walked past and we greeted one another on shabbas.

She was a refined young lady who always beamed a beautiful and bright smile. I am thinking of her and her family every day and pray that Hashem grants Lauren and the family much comfort and strength at this difficult time.'

Liora, aged 8

LLL: 4 May 2016

'Dear Rosenberg family.

Today was a bittersweet, humbling and devastating day, witnessing dear Liora (z'l) being laid to rest. We cannot ever understand why these things happen but seek comfort in other things, memories, legacies, symbols and the love and compassion that is shared by all whose life was touched by the light of Liora.

Today was indeed a very symbolic one. As the sun was shining gloriously, and I was standing there in silence amongst the massive crowd who came, it occurred to me that she was being buried in light. Every other funeral that I have attended the weather was melancholic and grey. Today was different, it was Liora's wave of light, her reassurance that there will still be light, and she will continue to send it.

All my love, and wishing you long life, peace and light xxx'

Painted by Liora, aged 10

AJK: 2 May 2016

'Donating platelets in the merit of Liora may she look down upon us and take care of her family and friends. Wishing all a long life.'

LW: 2 May 2016

'Do a mitzvah/good deed in the merit of Liora Rosenberg – Leah Rachel bat Sheftil Chaim,* a beautiful 20-year-old girl from Hendon who touched and inspired the lives of so many people around the world in such a short period of time. Liora's job in this world is now complete, and she is shining her continued light, energy and inspiration down on us.

Please keep posting your mitzvahs/good deeds, thoughts and inspirational words of support to the Rosenberg family. They need us now more than ever. Liora's dream before she passed was to help raise money to buy an ambulance for Hatzolah to replace the one that recently crashed. Please do whatever you can to help make this happen.'

https://www.justgiving.com/fundraising/liorarosenberg

CC: 1 May 2016

'Liora you lit the World up with your laughter, aspirations and heart. I'm lucky to have known you. Shine brightly darling.'

LS: 1 May 2016

'Today I was volunteering at Tikun making sandwiches for the homeless as part of Club Sandwich and JFriends and thought of Liora as I was doing this mitzvah. 🖤 💗'

---

* When a person passes on, the name reverts back to her original name 'Leah Rachel' and the tradition is that the mother's name 'Esther' is changed to the father's name, 'Sheftil Chaim'. The name of the Facebook group couldn't be changed to reflect this because of its size.

Liora with her grandparents in Strasbourg

HW: 1 May 2016

'Your strength is contagious, and courage is doing what we never thought we could do, doing it despite the fear, despite the dread, despite the pain and heartache. Hope can be given to others. It gives us strength and courage, and then hope grows. I wish the entire Rosenberg family a long life filled with hope, strength and courage. I hope that there will be no more tzorres [worries] and that Liora's light will shine upon you and all of Klal Yisrael [the Jewish People]. I hope that we can all continue to unite but for happy times. I and all my family are so very sorry for your loss.'

LW: 1 May 2016

'BDE Chaya Leah Rachel bat Sheftil Chaim.* Thank you to everyone who came together to pray for Liora and show Liora's family your support by doing mitzvahs/good deeds and posting inspirational stories of miracles. I saw many miracles happen this week because of Liora, and, even though she was not awake, she woke up over 15,000 people and brought us together as one big family, when we needed it the most […]. I had the pleasure of meeting you Liora, but I know many didn't, but they still loved you and we were all fighting for you to get better. May we merit to be even a fraction of your beautiful neshama [soul] which emulated chesed [giving]. You were an inspiration to the people you touched. May your soul be elevated, and your smile light up the sky. We are with you Liora, you will always be in my thoughts. Sleep well xxx'

Liora at Marcelle and Neil's wedding

---

*   The name 'Chaya' was added which means 'life'.

CR: 1 May 2016
'…happiness to all who see it. That's what Liora did the past two weeks – she brought a big light to the world, a light that brought redemption and happiness to numerous people around the globe, me amongst them. So, thank you Liora for letting me be involved in your Olam Haze [this world] story, and thank you Rosenberg family for introducing me to her most beautiful, redeeming, full of happiness light.'

Lauren Rosenberg: 30 April 2016
'Please, please, Liora is still on the life-support machine but they stopped her noradrenaline, so her blood pressure is dropping fast. She needs all of you to send her your love and healing right now please…'

NF: 30 April 2016
'I am getting married tomorrow and Liora will be in my thoughts and prayers.'

LW: 28 April 2016
'The beautiful Rosenberg family today. Miracles have happened every day, I have seen them with my own eyes. Let's do it again! Let's help Liora, and may we be granted a big miracle.

Please post your photos, messages of encouragement and good deeds and what country you are from and show the family your love is coming from all around the world.'

Lauren Rosenberg: 28 April 2016
'Please pray now they are doing the test now. Liora needs to show she can move…'

DB: April 28, 2016

'The boys wanted to write in the sand for Liora.'

LW: 27 April 2016

'*Chaya Leah Rachel bat Esther* every single one of you have helped to make little miracles happen.

Liora is still with us despite the doctors saying she wouldn't be over a week ago. We need a big miracle today.

A very important meeting is happening at 10am this morning and we are asking you to do whatever you can in prayer and mitzvahs/good deeds for a positive outcome. Liora is a fighter; we know she is still with us. We are asking you to fight with us too.

The family can't express how amazing the nurses have been. Now we have to help these nurses and help Liora and send her a shower of love and a quick and complete recovery.

Please only post words of encouragement and inspiration today. The family have asked that there is no press, tv or petitions, just love and positivity. Please show the Rosenberg family our strength and love by changing your picture in support. Miracles can happen, miracles DO happen. Praying for a miracle. #pray4liora'

The heart-shaped logo created by Liora's sisters

SG: 22 April 2016

'My amazing friend from Australia gave blood – incredible mitzvah in the name of Chaya Leah Rachel Bas Esther – with Shoshana Berger.'

Liora at 9 months reading Mother & Baby magazine

Other messages

We also received lots of other wonderful messages in many forms; here are just a few of them. They all meant a lot to us.

GL

'To family Rosenberg,

I've never met any of you, or beautiful Liora, but I don't think I've ever cried so much over the fight of someone I've never known. Liora touched me, and so many others, in the most powerful way which could only be because of her special shining Neshama. May Hashem comfort you and give you strength in this devastating time. Wishing you all a long life free from anymore heartache.'

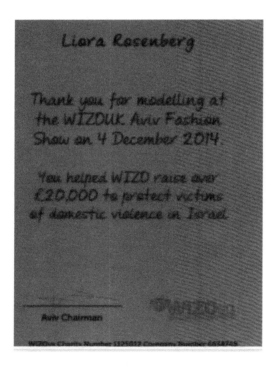

Thank you note to Liora for participating in a charity event

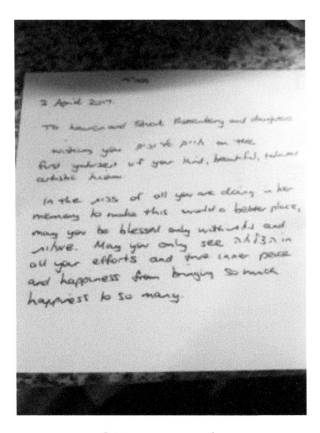

Letter sent anonymously

DF

'Dear Lauren,

Like many of us I don't really know what to say because there are no words.

I heard about what happened to Liora through Facebook, and only know you from Facebook groups, however we have 'spoken' about my daughter's anxiety issues and hypnotherapy in December.

From the first moment I heard, I could not stop thinking about you and your family and what you were all going through. I have been part of Tehillim ['Psalms'] groups in the past for friends and their children when there has been an extreme situation. I like to think that the Tehillim do work and believe that whatever the outcome the path for the person suffering is made easier. I have never spent so much time in personal prayer or wanted the Tehillim to work more than I have ever done in the last couple of weeks, but it was not to be.

I am certain that Liora's path has been made easier, and her Neshama is at peace partly because of the intensity of positive thought, mitzvot carried out around the world and tzedakah [charity] given in her merit.

I will treasure my daughters (21 & 19) more than ever, and hold them close, as none of us know what is around the corner. I do not know you and your family, and so do not want to intrude any further, suffice to say that Liora has made an impact on me and I will never forget. Wishing you and your family long life and that you all hold your memories of Liora in your hearts for a lifetime.'

SB

'I never met your daughter, but the waves of love I have seen during this sad time show that she was an incredibly special person who lived her life in a way we can all admire, a person who enriched the world and whose short life was incredibly meaningful. Her passing must leave you utterly bereft, and I am genuinely sorry for your loss. I wish you continued strength and love.'

Cake made by Fiona for Liora's birthday

ANONYMOUS

'Liora's story touched thousands of us. Although many of us didn't know the Rosenberg family at all, we'd seen Lauren post in our Mum group, and from the very first post about what had happened to her beloved daughter, we felt so much for her, for Liora and for all the family and we wanted to do whatever we could.

As a mum of two young girls I could only imagine with anguish how unbearable the last two weeks have been for you all. I have prayed for Liora alone, with friends, and with my two daughters, but always together with thousands of people who have all been touched by what has happened and hoped beyond hope for a different outcome to this.'

SG

'On reading last night that this was tragically not going to be the case, I can only hope that Liora's Neshama is at peace, and that she is a bright shining new star in the sky above us, where she will always be looking down on you all. My thoughts are with the family at this devastating time. Sending love and prayers that you will all be spared from any further sorrow.'

HM

'Dear Lauren

Words cannot even express how sorry I am. Your beautiful Liora, who I was not privileged enough to meet or know, touched us all. She inspired the world with her special sparkle, her strength and beauty.

And you, Lauren, inspired us too, with your love, unwavering faith, determination and hope. I think you are amazing, truly amazing. I wish you much love and strength at this unimaginably difficult time.

The whole world is wrapping their arms around you with love for your daughter. In her name you have made this world a better place.'

AE

'To Lauren and family

Words can't express the grief you must feel, but your angel has spread her wings and is now flying high and above and watching down on us.

Rejoice and celebrate a life so beautiful. May she be at peace and with you also.'

DB

'Dear Lauren and family

I just wanted to let you know that Liora touched people far and wide at a time when Bnei Yisrael are remembering our exodus together. Liora managed to bring 15,000 of us all together praying for one goal. She brought meaning to the word Achdut [Unity]. I hope during this time you will continue to see the Achdut she brought along with all the Chessed [giving] acts performed in her name.

You have every right to be truly proud parents, and no one can ever take that from you. May Hashem comfort you all amongst the mourners of Zion and may her Neshama have an Aliyah.'

KR

'Dear Lauren and Family,

Many heartfelt thoughts for you all on the loss of Liora. You are all in my thoughts and prayers, but I want to leave you with the words of poet Ellen Brenneman *(see next page)*.'

'We cannot know why the lily has so brief a time to blossom,

In the warmth of sunlight kiss upon its face,

Before it folds into its fragrance and bids the world goodnight

To rest its beauty in a gentler place

But we can know that nothing that is loved is ever lost,

And no one who has touched a heart can really pass away,

Because a beauty lingers on in each memory of which they've been a part.'

KR xxx

LW

'Dear Facebook Sister,
        You and your family are in my thoughts and prayers. I'm so very sorry for your loss.'

Family photo taken at Adina's batmitzvah

CHAPTER 11
HONOURING LIORA'S WISHES

There are many projects that honour Liora's wishes. If you think you or anyone else could help with any of them, please get in touch via www.fear-busters.com

Liora's Flower Gemach
Flowers4Shabbat

1: Flower Gemach
A weekly distribution of flowers to those having a difficult time. If you'd like to donate flowers or can connect us with a supplier who could help us to expand this work nationwide, please get in touch.

2: Raising funds for a Hatzola ambulance
Liora admired the work of Hatzola, who provide a rapid first response to medical emergencies in the community. We have raised money to help fund Hatzola's first rapid response ambulance.

Hatzola Rapid Response Ambulance

3: Other projects
Below are some projects we would like to accomplish:

- Selling Liora's artwork, in her memory.

- Establishing a charity called 'Light' to help fund therapy for those affected by difficult circumstances.

- Putting on an art exhibition.

- Setting up an official Art Day in UK schools.

- Putting into action a unique idea Liora had involving cars.

Liora travelling

HOW TO WORK WITH LAUREN

I hope after reading this book you will want to move forward and take further steps to leading a more fulfilling life. I've listed below some additional products and services which can give you extra knowledge, motivation and support. Sometimes we all need extra help and usually we achieve more when working with others rather than working alone.

Services

Workshops, courses and coaching

Check my website: www.fear-busters.com or details of my workshops, online courses, VIP days and coaching programmes. These can help you change your mindset to burst through your fears and boost your happiness and grow your business. Group work and one-to-one sessions are available face-to-face and via Skype or Zoom.

Speaking

I would be delighted to be asked to speak at your event, retreat or to your group at school or work.

Training

Let me know if you would like to be trained by me in one of the holistic techniques or know more about using essential oils. (Online classes are available).

Facebook Group

Join the Love, Light and Liora Facebook group: www.facebook. com/groups/LoveLightandLiora/

Daily Positive Affirmations for Teenagers

Take a look at the '366 Daily Positive Affirmations for Teenagers' Calendar via Amazon, which Liora originally designed.

Testimonials

Anxiety and Unhappiness

Health-related anxiety

Before seeing Lauren, I was anxious about my health and found it difficult to relax properly. The sessions with Lauren and techniques she taught me have made me feel much calmer, happier, and I have a more positive outlook in life.

When I met Lauren, I had several issues that needed working through, and all of them were very overwhelming. I had seen therapists in the past, and I had spent weeks talking to people about my problems and issues, and never getting very far.

I was sceptical, when I first met Lauren, about the methods she used but over time I started to trust the process, the techniques she used and allowed myself to go with it.

We have worked on small issues as well as very big ones. I always thought I would be the same person with the same issues and challenges, but Lauren's work has transformed my life in many ways. I am definitely a different, calmer person now, than when I first met her.

Lauren has allowed me to move on from the person I didn't want to be, to lose emotional baggage from the past and allow me to move forward in my life. She has helped me to rid myself of past hang-ups and not let the past define me.

She has shown and taught me skills and techniques to deal with day-to-day stresses and strains, and they have become almost second nature to me that I now reach for them as and when I need some extra support.

Lauren is kind, caring, non-judgemental and always wanting to help and support you. She believes passionately in what she does and wants to share that with her clients. She invests time in her learning and looking for new ways and techniques to help those 'in need' along their paths....

Child's depression

I contacted Lauren Rosenberg as I was desperate to find out what was going on with my son. He was depressed, unhappy, and feeling very low and disconnected, lost his confidence and had no energy. I didn't expect much, as I had no idea how Lauren works, but I was blown over with her level of success. The difference in my son's behaviour after only one session was unbelievable! I cannot explain in words how good we all feel as a family after seeing Lauren.

As I said to Lauren: 'Thank you so much, I have my son back. It is amazing.'

In an ideal world I would go and see her myself, and every member of my family for the rest of my life and of course will recommend her with no hesitation!

Self-expression

Lauren has seen both of my daughters and to say that she has had a positive impact on our lives is an understatement. She is kind beyond measure, and so wise and intuitive. She uses a range of techniques to help my young daughters (in our case we are navigating our way through the aftermath of a divorce), and she has really helped them express themselves, which in turn has helped me give them what they need. My eldest daughter had a fear of staying away from me, and, after a few sessions with Lauren, she is a different child, happy, much more relaxed and will happily stay out. My younger daughter is going through the process now, and, through Lauren, she is really coming on and able to express herself so much better. I can't recommend Lauren highly enough. Both girls look forward to their session, and Lauren is kind, understanding and gentle with them.

I found Lauren by chance, when a friend I'd asked to Google EFT practitioners in North West London found her and she lived just 3 miles away! I found her to be caring, considerate and totally non- judgemental of my issues. I met with her a few times and certainly noticed a difference, even though I was a total beginner.

I would thoroughly recommend Lauren if you suffer with panic attacks, anxieties or fears. I now rely on tapping as an ongoing tool when I'm worried or anxious about anything that life throws my way.

Try it, it works!

Feelings of guilt

Thank you for your helpful sessions. You've helped me to see things so differently, enabling me to feel much more positive, and most importantly have a real sense of freedom from all my worries. I can feel that burden of guilt and responsibility has been lifted off me.

Fear of dying

We took our daughter (7) to see Lauren as she suffered from fear of dying. We were very sceptical about the methods she used, but within a few sessions saw a radical change with our daughter's behaviour. I would definitely recommend people trying this method as it helped us very much.

Lack of confidence and self-esteem

I had a few sessions with Lauren relating to lack of self-esteem and self-confidence, as well as being upset. I feel hugely better. The treatment was the closest I have seen to a miracle cure. I'm just amazed at how sure of myself I am today. Honestly, I feel like a different person.

Sadness

Before we started working together I always felt sad, even when times were good. Lauren helped me finally get over the deaths of my best friend's baby 17 years ago and my Nana 10 years ago.

We also dealt with a distressing operation I had five years ago, and my unconscious fears about whether I could have a healthy child of my own one day.

She is a warm and gentle person, extremely good at what she does and the saviour of my sanity! I will be eternally grateful to her and recommend her to as many people as possible.

Stress

I have had the most incredible experience that has changed my life. Usually in therapy one or two sessions are spent on past experiences and current problems, so I knew I was on the right track when I was asked to complete a form before the session.

In the first session Lauren and I went straight to work, and it only took half a further session for me to obtain the full benefit of the therapy. I am amazed how quickly it worked and how much it helped me. I have no hesitation to recommend Lauren to anyone who has a deep-rooted problem or who just is going through a hard time and needs an extra boost.

Anger

I want to tell you of my very positive experience with Lauren. I went to see if she could help a member of my family who has a phobia but, as the hour went on, realised she could help me with my life as well. I travel quite a lot and it's very unsettling. I was often sad, pretty upset and cross with my way of life over which I have no control. In addition, menopause made me eat at strange hours and I didn't sleep well at night.

Lauren helped me time after time with anger, sleepless nights and so on. I am so much more relaxed, philosophical about my lifestyle, and much more patient with people who upset me. And I sleep so well now. My life is much happier and calmer thanks to Lauren, her understanding of human behaviour and her skills and helping

BLANK PAGE FOR YOUR NOTES

BLANK PAGE FOR YOUR NOTES

BLANK PAGE FOR YOUR NOTES

BLANK PAGE FOR YOUR NOTES

THE TREE OF LOVE AND LIGHT

Thank you to all those who have dedicated a leaf on this tree

A MESSAGE FROM LAUREN

Throughout this book I have tried to emphasise the importance of loving unconditionally and moving forward. I hope I've also shown you how being an energist and working with positive energy has helped me deal with the trauma of Liora's sudden illness and death. My final message to you is to remember to focus on the solutions, not the problems. Look for what will help you move forward and bring you support along the way.

If you have found this book useful, why not recommend it to a friend?

Best Wishes

Lauren

ABOUT THE AUTHOR

Lauren Rosenberg is an International Fear and Phobia Relief Expert, modern stress management coach, Reiki master and practitioner, qualified holistic therapist, mindset expert, trainer and energist who lives in London.

Born in France, Lauren studied History and History of Art at the University of Strasbourg. In 1991 she came to the UK to improve her English with a view to working at the European Parliament on her return to France. However, she liked it so much she stayed, then met her husband Stuart and had five wonderful girls.

She began training as a therapist in 2011 and now uses her many skills to help people overcome fear so they can move forward to lead more fulfilling lives.

Lauren uses a range of techniques, including Modern Energy Techniques, Theta Healing, Reiki, Colour Therapy, Positive Mindset and Integral Eye Movement Therapy. She has created her own unique therapy formula so she can provide more support and positive outcome to both adults and children.

Lauren discovered Essential Oil Therapy after Liora passed away but it helped her whole family. So, if you'd like to know more, go to www.mydoterra.com/laurenrosenberg/#/

Lauren felt compelled to write this book so she could share her story following the sudden passing of her eldest daughter, Liora. She also shares her knowledge and key messages through speaking engagements, online programmes, group work and one-to-one work.

Lauren believes:

'Energy is mystical and magical'

You can find out more about Lauren's work and the services she offers at www.fear-busters.com

999

808

(NB: These numbers are not a mistake. They are energy numbers and if you wish to know more Lauren will be more than happy to discuss it with you).